HOW TO TRY

Design Thinking —— *and* —— *Church Innovation*

LORENZO LEBRIJA

CHURCH
PUBLISHING
INCORPORATED

Church Publishing
19 East 34th Street
New York, NY 10016

Cover design by Marc Whitaker, MTWdesign
Typeset by PerfecType, Nashville, Tennessee

Library of Congress Cataloging-in-Publication Data

Names: Lebrija, Lorenzo, author.
Title: How to try : design thinking and church innovation / Lorenzo
    Lebrija.
Description: New York, NY : Church Publishing, [2021]
Identifiers: LCCN 2021006779 (print) I LCCN 2021006780 (ebook) I ISBN
    9781640653474 (paperback) I ISBN 9781640653481 (epub)
Subjects: LCSH: Church work. I Church management. I Christian leadership. I
    Organizational change.
Classification: LCC BV4400 .L43 2021 (print) I LCC BV4400 (ebook) I DDC
    254--dc23
LC record available at https://lccn.loc.gov/2021006779
LC ebook record available at https://lccn.loc.gov/2021006780

With much love I dedicate this book
to the person who each day makes me
a better priest, a better person, and a better Christian,
to my husband Troy.

CONTENTS

Foreword   ix

Acknowledgments   xi

Introduction: Welcome to TryTank   1

CHAPTER 1. Design Thinking and the Church   9

Field Notes   15

CHAPTER 2. There's a "T" in "Team"   21

Field Notes   29

CHAPTER 3. Step One: Generating Insights   33

Sidebar: Getting Buy-In   56

CHAPTER 4. Step Two: Developing Ideas   59

Sidebar: The Adjacent Possible   73

CHAPTER 5. Step Three: Trying   75

Field Notes   94

CHAPTER 6. Warning: It Will Seem Long, and You Will Fail—
and That's Awesome!   101

Sidebar: Unlock Your Creativity   105

CHAPTER 7. Using This Book as a Leadership Team   109

Final Thoughts: Celebrating Experimentation   114

Let us pray.

O God of unchangeable power and eternal light: Look favorably on your whole Church, that wonderful and sacred mystery; by the effectual working of your providence, carry out in tranquility the plan of salvation; let the whole world see and know that things which were being cast down are being raised up, and things which had grown old are being made new, and that all things are being brought to their perfection by him through whom all things were made, your Son Jesus Christ our Lord; who lives and reigns with you, in the unity of the Holy Spirit, one God, for ever and ever. Amen.

Collect for the Ordination of a Priest
Book of Common Prayer, page 528

FOREWORD

The difference between time and eternity is that the temporal constantly requires innovation and change; the eternal does not. This book is grounded in the truth of this reality. Church is obligated by the temporal necessity to innovate, think, revise, and revisit. In short, the church is obligated to be an organized entity that is constantly "trying" new ideas. Hence, the need for a "try tank."

The Rev. Lorenzo Lebrija has an MBA; he comes with an understanding of the Business and Administration literature. He has been a CEO of Seraphic Fire & Firebird Chamber Orchestra, Miami's professional choral and orchestral ensemble. He served for a season at a major foundation and has an MDiv from General Theological Seminary. The result is a person who weaves together both theory and practice. As this book shows he knows the literature; he has a theoretical model of change that he wants to apply. Yet as a priest who has served several congregations, he also understands the distinctive challenges of congregations.

As Lorenzo explains, the work of "trying" must include a willingness to "fail." This is a text that invites risk-taking. One explores an idea; one makes the journey; one attempts to implement the strongest version of the idea. And if it does not work out, then that is okay. A failure is a learning. One's knowledge about what might succeed is enhanced because one knows of one trajectory that did not succeed.

It is important to stress that Lorenzo is not approaching the issue of "trying" from a secular vantage point. Although we can learn from the successes and failures of the business world, we do not "try" out of a desire to emulate or, in some self-indulgent way, to increase our "brand" awareness. Lorenzo gets it entirely that this is the work of eternity; this is the work of the Holy Spirit; and this work matters more than anything else that we can do. Lorenzo Lebrija really does believe that God is, that we are redeemed through Christ, and that the Holy Spirit wants to work on our lives as a potter works on the clay. This book comes out of a place of deep faith and commitment. All our "tries" come out of a place of passionate commitment to the transformative power of the Gospel.

As the reader works through this book some ideas will make more sense, be more attractive, to the reader than others. But this is in the nature of "trying." What might look to one person as trivial might be to another really significant. And given that the future is unknown to us all, we do not know which idea might be "transformative." In 1994, the British prime minister received a memo encouraging him to create an email address for the government, although, the advisor explained, it is unlikely that there would be much email traffic. Judging a significant development in the moment is always difficult. But the person who "tries" might well be the person who finds the twenty-first-century equivalent of email for the church.

In short, the future belongs to those who innovate. If we could just find a certain formula that works for all time, then life would be so much easier. But this is not the way the world operates. As circumstances change, so the old formula is no longer effective. This is the reason humanity is called to renew, rethink, and revive the old and find new ways of living into the present. This book is that invitation.

The Very Rev. Ian S. Markham, PhD
Dean and President
Virginia Theological Seminary
All Hallows' Eve 2020

ACKNOWLEDGMENTS

The old African proverb that "it takes a village to raise a child" can easily apply to more than just raising a child. In all that we do, we never really do it alone—it really does take a village.

Thank you to my family: Troy Elder, Lucy, Cristina Corral, Luis Salazar, Juan Carlos Lebrija, Norma Tonella, Juan Carlos, Bernardo, and Alonso. A few words of thanks to those who helped me get to where I am as a priest: Doug McCaleb, J. Jon Bruno, Susan Brown Snook, Michael Bell, Ian Markham, Kurt Dunkle, and Lisa Kimball. For those who saw versions of this book along the way and made it so much better: Penny Bridges, Andrew Durbidge, Troy Elder, Rachel Nyback, Colin Mathewson, and Sean Steele. From Church Publishing: Nancy Bryan, Wendy Claire Barrie, Jennifer Hackett, and Ryan Masteller.

And what a village we are!

INTRODUCTION:
WELCOME TO TRYTANK

Two weeks after the United States declared a national emergency over the COVID-19 outbreak, no one really knew much. The predictions were all over the place, and none of them were good. At one point, the White House mentioned that the number of dead in this country would be around 250,000, and that was on the optimistic side. The pessimistic number was more than a million. It is simply hard to try and wrap your mind around a quarter of a million people or more dying from anything. On the nightly news were the stories of the individual lives that made up such a number.

Embedded in those stories was the fact that because this disease was so contagious, family members could not be with their loved ones when they died. The sheer number of deaths meant that usually overworked hospital chaplains were simply unable to cover it all. What we were hearing was profoundly disturbing to the soul: people were dying alone, and there was nobody there to pray with them at the end.

On March 24, the Episcopal News Service carried a story about the Rev. Peter Walsh, rector of St. Mark's Episcopal Church in New Canaan, Connecticut. It turns out that Father Walsh was prevented from being at the bedside of two dying parishioners, and so he administered the sacrament[1] to them by telephone. It was a necessity of the moment and, for the dying person and their family, small comfort in a very difficult time.

---

1. A sacrament is an outward and visible sign of an inward grace, for example, baptism and Eucharist.

But little did I know that the seed had been planted.

A few days later during a Monday staff Zoom call, we were discussing how terrible this all was, and how helpless we in the church felt. A colleague made a passing comment to the effect of, "I wish we could mobilize more priests to be there at this time, but we can't even be there in person." And in my mind, it clicked.

The TryTank process usually begins with a question: "What if?" In this case, it was, "What if we created a national phone number that any hospital could call to get access to a priest any time, day or night?" And, since local clergy are overwhelmed trying to create their own digital churches from scratch, what if we mobilized retired clergy to help out in this ministry?

The following week, just seven days from that insight, we found the technology to do it, put out a call for volunteers, trained them, and began to get the word out about a new ministry, Dial-A-Priest. While the name "Dial-A-Priest" may seem flip or even crass, the goal was to find a name that someone could remember enough to Google it. The thinking is that while they may not be able to remember the phone number, if they remember the name, they could get to it. Within days we were on the news. From the *New York Times* to my local newspaper in Palm Springs, California, to the NBC station in Washington, DC, there was interest in this new way of doing something old. The number of volunteer clergy also swelled from the one hundred we needed to almost two hundred names filling out a wait list.

As the new ministry was getting off the ground, we made discoveries and adjustments: the disease was hitting nursing homes hard and they generally don't have chaplains; could we expand to offer them care? Since at the end of life patients were mostly intubated and unable to speak, could we offer pastoral care to the family members as well? And what about pastoral care to the hospital staff that was depleted by fighting a virus that in many cases they simply could not beat? We did all of that. We also bought ads on Facebook aimed specifically at nurses and doctors in hotspot areas. The calls were coming in.

But it was not the deluge of calls you'd expect compared to the need, so we investigated what might be happening. It turns out that for those for whom last rites matter a lot, it also matters who is giving them. Also, many hospitals were not willing to share a number they had not heard about before or vetted. What if it was some crazy outfit and the "priest" on the phone would say this whole thing was a punishment from God for their sins? In other words, where there was the most need, they could not (usually by policy) use Dial-A-Priest. As the pandemic raged on, not as many people were dying at the same moment, so existing chaplains and pastoral care givers were able to support the need.

By the time we closed the line down at the end of May, we had taken 243 calls totaling 13 hours, 45 minutes, and 30 seconds. While some calls were longer, most were about 3–4 minutes in length. And to those who called, pastoral care was provided.

Was this experiment a failure? If the measure is only that we wanted to help people at the time of death, then it was not a failure. Not perhaps as many as we had anticipated, but we did. We also proved that the church can go pretty quickly from idea to reality. Most significantly, we discovered the combined thousands of years of experience that's available from our retired clergy.

What you may not have noticed as I just recounted that story is that it followed a now-familiar path: a framework for trying things. Insights led to ideas that were then tried. It's not rocket science. It's three steps and creating a mindset that allows for these kinds of experiments to happen. And those steps can be taught.

That's what this book is about.

Innovation in the Church

Whenever I tell people that I run a laboratory for church growth and innovation they generally give me a funny look that says "I realize all the words you were saying are in English but I'm not sure they make sense in the order in which you just said them." Let's face it, the church is not known for being the most innovative institution out there. We are the stewards of a tradition that's two thousand years old. Even so, innovation in the church has and continues to happen.

At a recent gathering in New York, I was having a conversation about my work with the former archbishop of Canterbury, the Honorable Most Rev. Rowan Williams. We were discussing innovation and the church when at one point he looked very excited as he proclaimed, "The Nicene Creed was an innovation in the church and *that* was in the fourth century!" When Martin Luther wrote the *Deutsche Messe*, "The German Mass," in 1526, he was aiming to make it more accessible to churchgoers since most of them didn't speak Latin. It was also the introduction of tuneful and accessible hymns: more innovation. Even when Anglicanism proclaimed a "middle way" between the Roman Catholic Church and Protestant reforms, that, too, can be seen as innovation.

Innovation in the church isn't ancient history. It happens quite regularly at many churches. Every time someone in ministry asks, "What if . . . ?" they are setting themselves up to innovate. That is what innovation is, a new way of doing something.

Even Jesus talks about innovation. Sure, he didn't give a viral TED Talk, but he was very clear that we should explore new ways of doing things:

> Later, Jesus himself appeared again to his disciples at the Sea of Tiberias. This is how it happened: Simon Peter, Thomas (called Didymus), Nathanael from Cana in Galilee, Zebedee's sons, and two other disciples were together. Simon Peter told them, "I'm going fishing."
>
> They said, "We'll go with you." They set out in a boat, but throughout the night they caught nothing. Early in the morning, Jesus stood on the shore, but the disciples didn't realize it was Jesus.
>
> Jesus called to them, "Children, have you caught anything to eat?"
>
> They answered him, "No."

He said, "Cast your net on the right side of the boat and you will find some."

So they did, and there were so many fish that they couldn't haul in the net. (John 21:1–6 CEB)

I have often wondered if maybe Nathaniel had said, "Hey, why don't we try the right side?" and Peter responded, "No, we fish from the left side." "But why?" Nathaniel would ask. And Peter would give the answer every church member has heard throughout time, "Because we've always done it that way." It took the son of God to get that to change.

Jesus's invitation is still very much the same for us today. Not getting more people in church? Something's not working out the way you want? Then try the other side. Do something different. Innovate.

TryTank

TryTank is a joint venture between Virginia Theological Seminary and the General Theological Seminary. When the deans of both seminaries and I were dreaming up how to best help the church of the future, they knew they needed something new. We all had conversations about what the future might hold and how the church could prepare. At one point, we thought about a place that could come up with ideas to share with the church, as a way of advancing the conversation, something similar to a think tank. We needed a place that could come up with ideas but that could also try them out. So, something more like a . . . TryTank, a place to think, explore, innovate, and to try. And they asked me to lead it.

While I really (really!) wanted to do this, part of me was afraid. What if the expectations were too much? Toward the end of the meetings about the lab and my running it, I asked both Ian Markham, the dean of VTS, and Kurt Dunkle, the dean of GTS, how we would measure success. "How will we know in a few years if we succeeded?" I was afraid that they would say something like "Well, because we saved the church," or "We will have found a silver bullet." As much as I wanted this exciting new job, there was no way I was going to try to do *that*. Instead, their answers were perfect for the task: "We will be successful if we failed more often than we succeeded with our experiments," said one. The other added, "Because we will have tried hundreds of things." Fail often and just keep trying? I was *in*.

In January 2019, TryTank was launched. Since then, we have run or are in the process of doing over sixty experiments. We're failing at a 50 percent rate (which, according to one of my bosses, shows we're not pushing the envelope far enough). We have birthed two ongoing ministries that have now found new homes, and our work is just beginning.

We think of TryTank as a "proof of concept" lab. It's a place where we can ask "What if?" a lot. We also have conversations with others who themselves are asking those questions and just wanted to know they weren't crazy.

As I mentioned earlier, innovation is not a totally new thing in the church. But generally, these are the steps that one would take to innovate in the church.

1. Think of an idea; pray about it.
2. Form a committee and hold listening sessions.
3. Write a paper and go to a conference.
4. Do theological reflection.
5. Hear about how it was already tried in 1912.
6. Bring it to the vestry.
7. Since they said "No" the first time, bring it to the vestry again.
8. Try it.

This framework is how you end up with a MySpace[2] page in 2021.

In order to do this work in a way that makes sense, we developed a framework for how to try things. By developed, I mean that we looked

---

2. MySpace.com was a precursor to Facebook that was all the rage until Facebook came along and then completely killed them.

around at the many ways that the business world tries new things and we adapted one that worked well in our context. Our framework needed to be simple and nimble. It had to be quick and very organic. We looked at how the great consulting firm McKinsey & Co. does their work. We also considered the scientific method (being a lab and all). But they didn't fit. And we kept looking until one fit just right. We landed on design thinking with some adaptations for the church. (Don't worry that you don't know what design thinking is; we'll cover that shortly.) In the end, I think our framework is exactly all those things we needed and wanted.

In chapter 1, we'll look at design thinking as the framework we use. In chapter 2, we will cover how to put together a team to do this. In chapters 3–5, we will go through each of the three steps. In chapter 6, we will look at failure and those times you will want to walk away from this work, and why you should not. Finally, chapter 7 is about how to use this book as the guide for a congregation leadership retreat. Along the way, I will share with you some of our field notes, the stories of some the experiments that have worked and some that have not.

God at the Center

Before we get to all of that, there is one last point to cover here. While this work is exciting and fun, and we're learning from business and other disciplines, it is very important to remember that this work is about—and for—God. Ours is a God of creation who is always inviting us into new ways of being. Every step of the way should begin with a moment, spoken or not, when you and your team remember that this is holy work. Invite the Holy Spirit to be with you and guide you, and to open your hearts and minds.

It is my prayer that you will try many things and that in trying you will encounter the Holy Spirit who leads us and empowers us to do this work. May God bless you in it.

Design Thinking
and the Church

Design thinking is a process, but it started as a school of thought. In the 1960s, efforts in the corporate world were made to better inform the process of product design. Rather than just hoping that creative people would come up with new and innovative designs, was it possible that they were following a roadmap? This new field was called design research.

A Short History of Design Thinking

Design as a framework was explored in Robert A. Simon's 1969 book, *The Sciences of the Artificial*. Professor Robert McKim of Stanford made leaps in the nascent field in the 1980s and 1990s. During that time, it was recognized that the design of products needed to focus on the needs of the people who would use them, not only on the needs of commerce. That was the key element: it was centered on people first.

In 1987, Peter Rowe first popularized the term "design thinking" to encompass this method, and now it was able to go beyond products. Design thinking could be used to dream up experiences or figure out how to improve education. The core concepts were being applied in more and more fields. By the 1990s, David Kelley of the influential design firm IDEO was among the founders of what is now called the Design Thinking Movement. (FYI, when we launched TryTank in January of 2019, we sought out a framework to use for our work. After looking at several and trying a few, we settled on design thinking because it made sense for what we wanted to do. To really do it well, I was trained and certified by IDEO in this process in 2020.)

As it is currently used, design thinking is a process for creative problem solving. Or, to put it more academically, "Design thinking is a human-centered approach to finding real innovative solutions to tough problems. Design thinking combines the approaches of design, management and science to solving a wide range of complex problems . . . design thinking is about intelligent change."[1]

IBM was an early adopter of design thinking, creating their very successful IBM Enterprise Design Thinking innovation lab. So was MassMutual (yes, the insurance company) when they wanted to reach a new market. Fidelity Labs is the in-house lab of Fidelity Investments. Even Intuit, the company behind TurboTax, has Intuit Labs, which used design thinking once with eighth graders to create a social enterprise.

Today, design thinking has influenced more things than you could imagine. From toys and shopping carts and video games, to how kids are fed in a school cafeteria, it really is everywhere. I think this is so because it's an organic and intuitive way to creative problem solving and generating ideas.

---

1. Robert Curedale, *Design Thinking: Process and Methods* (Los Angeles, CA: Design Community College Inc., 2019), 12.

The Framework

Here are the three steps:

1. Generating Insights
2. Developing Ideas
3. Trying

See what I mean about it being an organic and simple process? I would bet that in many areas of your life you have used the design thinking process without even knowing it. You had an insight about something. The insight led you to think of ideas you could try. Then you tried one of them. Congratulations, you are a design thinking practitioner!

If it's so simple and you have already done it, why do you need this book? Because there are better ways of doing it. Imagine being better able to gain insights. Imagine being better able to come up with ideas. Finally, imagine being better equipped to try them. That's what this book is really about. (And quite frankly, even if you don't need to be better at this, the church does.)

Why Design Thinking Works for the Church

I believe design thinking is perfect for our holy work, especially if you are part of a liturgical tradition. We love to follow frameworks! But it goes beyond just that. Once, I was working with someone to carry out a new ministry in a congregation. It didn't take long for us to realize that we hadn't done a good job of getting buy-in from the congregation. Without the buy-in, some people felt hurt that they weren't in on the creation process and were unlikely to support it. It would be hard for the new ministry to become sustainable without support from the congregation. We found that this was going to be a longer process than we had anticipated. After noting that we were going to have to backtrack and get involvement from people, both of us let out a long sigh, and my partner in ministry said, "Doing the work of the people of God would be considerably easier without the people of God." We laughed. The process of design thinking as we have developed it for the church helps you get buy-in from stakeholders along the way.

I once had a boss who described how a new idea came to be by saying, "We threw a bunch of spaghetti at the wall and saw what stuck." That seems like a wasteful way of trying new things, and it's also a top-down way of coming up with ideas. Rather than gaining insight from those who would take part, it just "seemed like a good idea" and then it was pushed out. That process looks more like this:

1. Idea
2. Try

It's missing the key step of getting insights. When generating insights, what you are actually doing is clarifying the question your ministry is looking to answer. To put it another way, design thinking helps you be crystal clear about objectives.

Finally, design thinking maximizes your chance of success because you are not just throwing things at the wall and hoping they stick. The church doesn't have the resources or the time for that. We need to be much more intentional about what we're doing, and design thinking helps do that.

The Design Thinking Mindset

One of the best things that happens when you undertake design thinking as a process to lead change and innovation is that your mindset changes. You no longer just see things; you are always looking for those insights. At the same time, you are planting seeds in your mind that will grow and connect to those insights.

Remember when I talked about Dial-A-Priest? The seed that was planted was the news story about the priest who gave last rites over the phone. Somewhere, I had also learned about companies that were running call centers, but they were not in one large phone room anymore:

technology allowed the calls to be routed to the agent's own home. And then, when the insight came about the upcoming overwhelming need that was coming for pastoral care, my mind connected the dots into a "What if . . . ?"

I firmly believe that our minds naturally want to work this way. We do it every time we are creative. Steve Jobs, the founder of Apple, said, "Creativity is just connecting things. When you ask creative people how they did something, they feel a little guilty because they didn't really do it, they just saw something. It seemed obvious to them after a while." Scientists who study the brain have concluded that creativity requires the mixing and remixing of mental images in our brains that represent the external reality.[2] We can hone those mindsets and make them stronger.

Now, you are not going to become Sherlock Holmes and every time you walk into a room you'll automatically start to look for the smallest details, and how, and why things are, but you will notice things more. You will be more open and inquisitive about details. You will plant little seeds. Plant enough of them and they will grow. Your mind will make the connections.

In each of the steps, I list the mindsets that will be most helpful. For the insight step, the mindset is being curious. For the idea step, the mindset is being playful. For the trying step, the mindset is being courageous. Anyone, at any age, can work in these mindsets, and they are what open us to getting the most out of this work.

The Example We Will Use

In brain-speak, I am a left-brain kind of person. I am practical to the core. This is a great quality to have. Mostly. It is hard for me to follow some of the more theoretical and esoteric points of theology and

---

2. Melissa C. Duff et al., "Hippocampal Amnesia Disrupts Creative Thinking," National Library of Medicine (Hoboken, NJ: Wiley Periodicals, Inc., 2013).

philosophy. Some of my courses in seminary were very hard because of this. The professor (usually some very distinguished archbishop or the like) would be teaching a theory of the atonement and I'd be just lost. I would raise my hand and ask, "Can you give me a practical example of that?"

I say all that as a preface to what follows. I see it as very practical and I want to teach it that way. To that end, I want to use one example we can follow throughout the book that will let us use what we are learning in a practical way.

This is our scenario:

Sue is a new vestry[3] member of St. John's Episcopal Church. She's been a member of the congregation for about a year, maybe a little more. The church is an average Episcopal congregation. It has seventy people at worship on Sundays and about two hundred on the membership rolls. The members skew older, so while there are two or three families with small children, most of the members are at or near retirement.

Sue was recently elected to the vestry. At her first meeting, she asked about evangelism and efforts made by the church in trying to get new members. After a long discussion of the things the congregation had done in this area in the last thirty or so years, she agreed to head up a small group to look at this question: "What if we intentionally sought out new members?"

In design thinking, this is our design question. It is what leads our insights and ideas and our trying. Please note that the question will evolve. At a later point, there will be an intentional pivot to it becoming an action question.

It is very possible that as you begin this work, the design question itself will change as you gain more clarity. For example, this "What if we intentionally sought out new members?" could become "What if we intentionally sought out young families?" or "What if we intentionally

---

3. A vestry is the governing board of the congregation in Episcopal churches.

sought out LGBTQ members?" Don't be afraid of the pivots! They are good, they show that your insights are already bearing fruit and leading you to a more clear and specific question. Let that happen.

For now, we'll begin with the original question of "What if we sought out new members?" which we'll use as our example for the rest of this book. I hope that as we go along you will be better able to follow the process by the illustration of the example. I hope that you will also think of your own design question. Take some time now and think about some of the "What ifs?" you may have about your own congregation. Pray about them. Ask God to illumine your mind and heart to begin this work.

—— FIELD NOTES ——

Throughout the book, I'll share some of the experiments that TryTank has done, what we were hoping to achieve, and what actually happened. Not all of our experiments have been successful. Of our first fifty experiments, six have succeeded, fifteen have failed, and the rest are currently in process or are still in development.

Alexa Prayer Skill

Design question: How might we lower the barriers to get people to engage with scripture more regularly?

The idea: Research tells us that people who engage with scripture at least four times a week are more optimistic, more generous, gamble and drink less, and are less likely to have extramarital affairs. So, could we lower the barrier to make it easier for people to engage scripture on their own?

The smart speaker is perhaps the fastest adopted technology in human history. It took virtually no time to go from its introduction to more than a hundred million of them in the U.S. Within the category, the most widely used smart speaker is Alexa from Amazon, a small device that you interact with using your voice. Applications for the speakers are called "skills."

We set out to create a skill that people could access easily to play a four-minute version of Morning Prayer for them. We were limited to four minutes since those are the parameters set by Amazon unless you play a different kind of media. The other kind of media is more expensive to develop, so it's important to look for the minimum viable prototype to test before investing more.

A few weeks later, our skill was active, and once you enabled the skill for your speaker, you could say, "Alexa, open Episcopal Prayer," and she would respond with "The Lord be with you," followed by the prayer session. In just a few weeks we had dozens of people praying regularly with the speaker. We ran surveys and interviewed some of the users to evaluate the skill. People loved it. While it was not getting new people to pray the Daily Office, it was augmenting people's current prayers. Amazon even sent us a note calling it one of the "most engaged" skills, meaning that the same people were returning regularly. They were so impressed that users no longer had to activate the skill; it was now automatically available on every Alexa speaker. (Fun party trick: next time you're visiting a friend and they have an Alexa speaker, say, "Alexa, open Episcopal Prayer," and check out their reaction. It might also be why friends are not inviting me to visit. Hmmm.)

Once we proved the concept, we went to the next level with it. We partnered with Forward Movement, a publisher whose aim is to "empower disciples." They already produced a daily podcast of the Morning Prayer and would soon also provide an Evening Prayer podcast. We went back to our programmers and had them program the skill to access and play the podcast for either prayer based on the time of the day of the person asking. It worked beautifully. We also expanded from Alexa to the Google Assistant. Those two systems combined constituted the bulk of users in the U.S. Before we knew it, some five hundred people were regularly praying the Daily Office with the skill.

At this point, our part of the journey was complete. We asked Forward Movement if they would like to take over the new ministry and they agreed. They are now the proud owners of the skill, and we had birthed a new ministry into the church.

The experiment result: it worked!

Spin Church

Design question: How might we engage people who are finding their spirituality in group fitness classes?

The idea: Some people who are not going church are finding their sense of spiritual community in other places. After all, as spiritual beings, we yearn for that spiritual connection. One of those places is group fitness classes. If you have ever visited a Soul Cycle studio, you'll understand what I mean. When you walk into the studio, the lights are dim and there are lit candles all over the place. On the wall it reads "find your soul" and other similar statements. During the class, the instructor asks you to pedal harder and then says something like "There's no yesterday, there's no tomorrow, there's only this day that was created for you." When I saw and heard that, I thought, "Throw in a 'Jesus' or an 'amen', and you have yourself a pretty good sermon." So, the idea became, if people are finding their spirituality in group fitness classes like spinning, what if we took a spinning class and made it an actual spiritual event? And since we're liturgical people, how about a Eucharist? The Spin Church experiment was born.

We put out a call to find partner congregations and found one in Newport, Rhode Island. We then found a nearby spin studio that would rent us space on a Saturday late afternoon (the thinking being, this will be the vigil service!). We made some postcards and posters to pass around. We also bought some Facebook ads to plug Spin Church.

About those ads . . . We know that 26,799 unique people saw the ads and that they were 86 percent women and 14 percent men. Which is just what we wanted. Those nearly 27k people saw our ads 160,671 times, about 6 times each, on average. Nice! Of the 27k who saw the ads, 1,176 actually engaged with the ad. This means they "liked" or forwarded or clicked on the ad. That's a rate of 1.40, which is three times (!!) the Facebook benchmark for "well-performing" campaigns. Woo hoo! And we actually had nine people sign up for our class, which is great because it was a small studio and we were limited to about ten at any "service." But—yeah, you knew the *but* was coming—none of them ever showed up.

Since we had their contact information, we were able to connect with them to try to see what happened. It turns out that people who are finding their spiritual connection through group fitness classes are already finding their spiritual connection through group fitness classes. In other words, all we did was create a new option for them, and they already had a connection with one, so why change? It was no different than if we had just started a new church next to all the other churches and tried to get people to come to our new one (in which, by the way, the service is longer because it's a full class and then a Eucharist).

The experiment result: it did NOT work.

Here I am leading the Eucharist after the class. To my right is the deacon who, now that I look back, looks a little dubious! LORENZO LEBRIJA

There's a "T" in "Team"

I believe that Jesus was a smart guy, really smart and wise. As such, I think he was spot-on when he sent his disciples out into the world two-by-two. It wasn't that we couldn't do what was needed by ourselves; Jesus simply knew that we're always better working together.

Imagine that you are somewhere unfamiliar, maybe a foreign country where you don't even speak the language, and you are lost. It can be pretty scary. Now imagine the same situation but your best friend is with you. You are just as lost, but somehow it seems much more bearable, doesn't it? Jesus was right, two-by-two is better.

To do this work of trying, of bringing about change in our church, you do not want to do it alone. First, it'll be harder, and who wants that? Second, it won't be as good. Even the best ideas can be made even better when others add their part. Finally, if anything is likely to be sustainable and have a shot, then getting buy-in from others is essential. (That last one, by the way, is true in the church and in most places in life.) So, you'll want to put together a team to help you do the work.

Excitement

Before anything else, you want to make sure that all of the people on your team are excited by this process and what you can all learn and do together. This is paramount! This may mean that you'll have to search a bit more for team members, but it will be worth it.

Skills

You want to find people who have different skills than you do, to complement your own skills with the skills you lack. For example, if you are not that good at researching (and following the inevitable rabbit holes to find useful information is definitely a skill!), then it makes sense to find someone who is good at researching. Likewise, if you'd rather die a thousand deaths than speak in front of an audience, then find someone who can make excellent presentations, since the task of getting buy-in along the way will require them. Think carefully about the skills necessary to do the work and be honest with yourself about whether you have those skills, or if you need to find someone who does.

Roles

You'll also want to find people who can fill different roles on the team: someone to the do schedule to coordinate when people can meet, someone who will record what you are learning and make ongoing sense of it, someone to keep your meetings on time and on point, someone to keep track of expenses. Having a designated person for each role will make your team run like a well-oiled machine.

Diversity

One way that a team can add to even the best idea is by having different views of the same problem, opportunity, or data. In order to get the most perspectives, you'll want diversity among team members. Make sure that your team has age, gender, ethnic, cultural, and racial diversity. This is especially true if you are going to explore an area that is not represented in your congregation. Say that you wanted to find out how to reach more Hispanic members in your community. If your team has no Hispanic members, you're going to come up with limited answers that may not even be relevant to Hispanics. You'll need some Hispanic representation on your team. "But Lorenzo," you might say, "we don't have any Hispanics in our congregation; that's why we want to reach them!" Good point. Invite a Hispanic friend to be an ad hoc part of your team even if they are not currently a member of your congregation. If you don't have any Hispanic friends, then that should be your first step. Forget the team, go make some new friends.

Size

While there is no prescribed perfect size, there are some advantages to having between three and five members on your core team. Your core team is the one that gathers regularly to do the work. It's the team that should have a range of skills and has defined roles and is diverse. That said, there will be times when you want to expand the team for a specific task. Then you can invite people whom you trust to help with a one-time thing. Maybe you are in the idea phase and want to really get a rich set of possible ideas using a brainstorming technique; it would make sense for you to add a few more carefully selected people to help you.

In sharing your insights with new temporary members, you are clarifying those insights for your own team as well, and that can spur ideas. Second, since they have not been part of the process, what they bring to the table can be new and fresh and really outside of the box. Their questions can be worth gold! Finally, having other people participate will automatically give you other stakeholders in the process, which makes it easier to get continued buy-in and support.

Looking for a T team

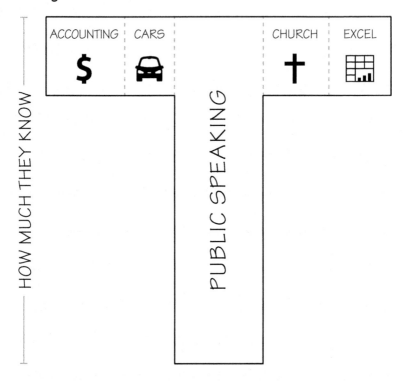

This illustration shows a person on a "T" team. They know a few things about accounting, cars, church, and Excel, but they know a lot about public speaking. This is what you want to be looking for in members of your team.

As you look around to put the team together (both the core and expanded team), you'll want to look for T people. These are people who have a wide range of skills (that's the upper horizontal bar of the T) *and* who have deep knowledge in one or two of those skills (that's the vertical bar of the T). This allows you to have more data. Insights come about when data points shine. So, the more data, the more likely that some will shine. You don't need everyone on the team to be MacGyver or Hermione Granger, who seem to know everything about all things. People who know a thing or two about a lot of things and then really know a few areas are the ones that can make the connections that help in this work.

Communication

Communication is one of the most important skills to hone and get right. By "get right" I do not mean that your prose should rival Shakespeare's or that your narrative is as gripping as a Pulitzer Prize–winning novel. Rather, effective communication boils down to two skills we can all improve on: managing expectations and using empathy.

Managing expectations

Every moment of our day, in everything we do, people we interact with have expectations of us. Most of the time these expectations are unspoken. To manage expectations, make sure that your team knows what's next and that they are not surprised by hearing something elsewhere they should have heard from you. Let's say a deadline was set for something to happen on the fifteenth of the month. Due to circumstances beyond anyone's control, that's not going to happen. If you let the team know up to the fourteenth that it's not going to happen as you all had agreed because of X, they will be okay with the change and move on. Don't wait. Why? Because then the deadline passed and the expectation was not met. You can only manage expectations before they happen. After, you are controlling damage.

When expectations are managed in advance, people are much more sympathetic and willing to help search for alternatives. Once when I was working in arts management, on the night of a concert I realized that the piano tuner was running behind and we were not going to be able to open the doors thirty minutes before the concert as we normally did. Ten minutes before that deadline, I went out to the lobby, stood on a chair, and asked for their attention. There staring at me were several hundred people who had paid good money for their tickets. I told them what was happening and that in order for the piano to be tuned well, the hall needed to remain empty while it was tuned. I apologized and said I understood that standing outside was uncomfortable but that we'd get them in as soon as possible. After I got off the chair and was walking back toward the box office, everyone I passed told me that it was fine and not to fret. I guarantee you that if I had done that even one minute past 7:30 p.m., they would not have felt the same. Managing the expectations worked. But did you notice the other thing I did? By telling them that I understood that they were uncomfortable, I also was empathetic to their situation, which is the second key to effective team communication.

Using empathy

We as a society undervalue the importance of empathy in our lives. When we can show someone that their situation matters, it shows them that we care. Often, this can be done without even having to say, "I care about your situation." It's about being careful in *how* we say what we say.

A few years ago, I realized that I got better responses to my emails when I removed most personal pronouns. Instead of saying "you" or "I," I'd look for more generic terms that were more inclusive, like "us" or "we." Likewise, when requesting something, when I reworded demands as requests I was much more likely to get a positive response. Perhaps it has to do with how our brains process things. This is one way you can ask for clarity:

> *Sue, I was reviewing your submission for the newsletter and I have no clue what you're trying to say in the second paragraph.*

But that sounds a bit abrasive, doesn't it?

Sue, thanks for the on-time submission for the newsletter. Can you help clarify the second paragraph? Is this still about the interviews? It seems like the reader might get lost.

The second email takes out the personal pronouns, and then begins by thanking the volunteer (we don't do that nearly often enough, so any opportunity is a good opportunity to do so). Then it asks for more clarity. Sue can reread her own work and ask a follow up question or rewrite. Empathy about how the critique might be received defused the automatic defense that could have come up.

We really like the speed of email, and while that is one of the great things about it, most of the time this "need for speed" means we do not reread our emails before sending them. We generally write and hit send. Taking just a moment to reread and rephrase can prevent headaches and allow for better responses. When your team feels informed and that they are indeed part of a team, you're well on your way.

Sharing back to the team

Aside from keeping the team informed outside of meetings, I want to talk about something that is an important part of each of the three steps: sharing back to the team.

For much this work, you will either be in teams of two or by yourself. You might conduct conversations in teams so that one can take notes and the other one conducts the actual conversation. In looking at secondary sources like articles or studies, you will likely do that by yourself. The whole team will not always be present and you will have to report to the others about what you found. When sharing back, keep in mind that you are looking for insights and stories always work best.

Insights

What is a good insight? An insight is an "Aha!" moment, but that does not mean that you must be on the lookout for earth-shattering, eureka moments. It's more subtle than that. What you are looking for is something that caught your interest. You do not yet have to see or know how or if it connects to something else. Many—even most—times, it won't. But remember that you are planting seeds. At this stage, just jot it down and know that it's interesting.

In design thinking, a good insight has three qualities: First, it informs. It's something you didn't know before and it's interesting. Second, a good insight inspires. The insight can motivate you to *do* something. When I first thought about Dial-A-Priest, the insight that motivated me was knowing that last rites could be done over the telephone. Somewhere in my mind I had planted the seed that the technology existed for dispersed call centers, but it was when I learned a new insight that the dots connected in a new way. Finally, a good insight is memorable. It sticks in your mind and is something you can easily share.

Not all insights meet all three criteria. Just remember that you are looking for those "hmm, that's interesting" bits. Don't start judging it now or trying to see how it all connects in. For now, "interesting" is very, very good. (These tidbits are also great at parties. When I was in high school in the 1980s, for the longest time I kept a little nugget of information I had read in *Harper's Index*: there were "forty-eight Jews in Hong Kong." I found that just amazing. It was a bit useless for, well, just about anything. But to me, it was incredibly interesting, and I used it at parties all the time.)

In sharing back, stories always work best. Remember that line from *Dragnet*, "Just the facts, ma'am"? Well, forget about it. If you are recounting something that someone told you in a conversation, tell them the story of the insight, not just the facts. Like my anecdote about Jews in Hong Kong. It was likely more memorable to you as a story than if I had just mentioned that I once recounted at (very few) parties that there were forty-eight Jews in Hong Kong. (Just because I want you to be well-informed, according to the World Jewish Congress there are now about 2,500 Jews in Hong Kong.) Remember that stories work!

—— FIELD NOTES ——

Latino Ministry in a Box

Design question: How might we allow congregations with no Spanish-speaking clergy to reach their nearby Hispanic[1] neighbors and make community?

The idea: The demographics of the U.S. are changing, and fast. Projections[2] tell us that by 2045 the US will become minority white. The largest minority making up the new majority will be Hispanics. The Episcopal Church, however, is 90 percent white and only 2 percent Hispanic.[3] The biggest problem faced by congregations all over is that, while they see their neighborhood changing, they don't speak Spanish and don't know how to connect with their Hispanic neighbors. What if there was a systematic approach that could guide these congregations in the process of reaching out to Hispanics and that

1. The term "Latino" is shorthand for "Latinoamericano," which is someone from Latin America. "Hispanic" refers to those who come from a Spanish-speaking country. There are several countries in Latin America that do not speak Spanish (Brazil, for example).
2. William Frey, "The U.S. Will Become 'Minority White' in 2045, Census Projects," The Brookings Institution, March 14, 2018, https://www.brookings.edu/blog/the-avenue/2018/03/14/the-us-will-become-minority-white-in-2045-census-projects/.
3. "Members of the Episcopal Church," *Religious Landscape Study*, Pew Research Center, https://www.pewforum.org/religious-landscape-study/religious-denomination/episcopal-church/, accessed February 18, 2021.

provided them all the tools to make this happen? And with regards to language, what if this "system" took care of that need, too?

One of the most common ways to plant a church in a new place is to start by making relationships and then after you have a few, lead a Bible study. It's a method that works and that was our model for this experiment. We would provide flyers to attract people to a new Spanish-language Bible study. For the Bible study itself, we'd provide a curriculum, handouts (even for kids!), and a recorded video in Spanish that, in a sermon-type way, would explain the Bible passage. Basically, every necessary piece would be provided to the congregation: *Latino Ministry in a Box.* All they had to do was find a bilingual lay leader that could lead the Bible study and engage with the people who came.

The longer-term goal was that the Bible study would run for a period of time, say six months. During that time, some of the members would naturally invite friends to join. So, while there might be four or five people at the first gathering, in six months maybe there would be twelve. And at the end of the first year, there would be twenty. That's a community! During this time, the priest could learn the six paragraphs of the Eucharistic Prayer in Spanish from *El Libro de Oración Común* (The Book of Common Prayer). By the time there's a community, the Bible study could become a mostly lay-led eucharistic service.

We tested the system in eight congregations[4] around the country during Lent, since it was a short liturgical season that has a nice end point. Each week we provided all of the elements to the congregations, and each week, they'd report back on how things

---

4. One of the partner congregations already had a Spanish-language ministry, but the priest didn't feel confident in Spanish. We wanted to find out if people would welcome a well-crafted sermon through video. It worked, too! And it took that burden from the priest.

were going. It didn't take long to notice it was working. Although it was intended to be an hour, the Bible studies were taking an hour and a half or two. People were sharing. We saw reports that the discussions were so rich that they couldn't finish the agenda. And— the best part as I saw it—people started to bring food! Community began to form.

When we reported out on this, there was a lot of excitement. Of course, we learned how to make it better in the evaluation process (add English subtitles to the videos so that others can be present, and welcome the new members or take a little longer to build relationships before starting the Bible study). In the end, three dioceses came together to take over the ministry. They will try it out for a longer period to make sure it really works and then they want to offer it as a ministry to the whole church.

The experiment result: it worked!

TryTank at Comic-Con

Design question: How might we learn more about younger people who have no religious affiliation (the "Nones")?

The idea: As you probably have noticed, we at TryTank like to delve into the research. It really is a good place to find insights that you can then explore by ideating and trying. One of the areas that presents opportunity for the church is in how to reach out to younger folks who are not that into church. The research firm Barna reports that from 2011 to 2019, the number of church dropouts rose from 59 percent to 64 percent of eighteen-to-twenty-nine-year-olds.

So, what if we went to the annual Comic-Con convention in San Diego and got a booth? Just spend four days having conversations where we could ask young people about their lives, their desires, and aspirations. Could we glean new insights that might lead to new experiments we could try? After all, the annual convention gets about 180,000 attendees, and they are all fans of moral stories (notice that most comic books are moral stories of the battle between good and evil). Although it would be long days of hard work, we felt that the potential of what we could learn was huge.

We applied for a booth and started to work on how we would brand ourselves there to show that we really do value the attendees' opinions and wanted to learn. As we progressed in our plans, we got a note from the producers of the event saying, "Thanks, but no thanks." They have a policy that does not allow religious organizations to exhibit at the convention. I was shocked at first, but then I realized, they probably only put such a policy in place if they have had some sort of bad experience in the past, right? I am guessing that once upon a time a religious organization maybe did get a table and what they had to share was condemning of the people there? Maybe they talked about how comics were evil? I don't know, but it ended the experiment for us.

And this brings up a good point. Sometimes an experiment will fail through no fault of your own. Some things are completely out of our control. All you can do is try to figure out if there's a way to pivot and make it something else or, as we did here, to call it a day.

The experiment result: it did NOT work!

3

STEP ONE:
Generating Insights

The mindset for this step: Be curious.

I believe that humans are, for the most part, curious creatures. All you have to do is spend some time with a kid and you will hear a litany of questions asking the "why" of everything. I really think it's just part of how we are made. That is good, because it is the mindset of curiosity that will lead us to find insights.

It is possible that your church leadership team may not be thinking in this way yet. That's okay. If you bring some questions to them when starting the process of talking about this, you can prime the pump to show by example what you mean, and also that it's not as hard as they may be imagining.

The Design Question

Before we can look for insights, we need to at least be pointed in the right direction. Otherwise we might as well just open Google and stare at it. Much like that Google search bar, we need a starting query to point us somewhere. As you dig deeper, the question will evolve and might change altogether, but it'll be based on those insights. That means it's changing intelligently. But we're getting ahead of ourselves.

You'll recall that the question we are using as an example is: "What if we intentionally sought out new members?" The question is only a starting point. It will evolve. Looking around at your own context, what challenges is your congregation facing that may call for a new approach? Here are some examples of questions you may be asking:

Should we add a contemporary service?
How can we better serve our neighborhood as it changes?
Should we open a preschool?
How can we bring in more revenue?

All of those are valid questions and each represents a challenge that would be worthy of a deep dive that design thinking can facilitate. The only thing your design question must do is point you in some direction.

Many congregations get to the question and then jump right to the second step, the idea part. You may have even done it yourself; I know I have. This is tempting. We think that knowing the question is enough to "get to work." The question is the direction you are headed, which is a start, but not as useful as it could be. It's like deciding that "How do we go west?" and then we immediately say, "It's that way, get in the car, let's go!" And off we go. With the insight step, we can go from "How do we go west?" to "How do we go to Los Angeles?" Now, you have more options and you are much clearer on where you are going. You even have choices as to the mode of transportation! This alone will make a significant difference in the work of your congregation.

Once you have a question in hand, now you are ready to find some insights. Good insights inform, inspire, and are memorable. There are many (many!) ways to seek insights. We are going to cover four of them here. These are the four that TryTank uses regularly in our work. They are secondary research, observation, conversation, and empathy experience.

Secondary Research

If you read a news report recently, then you have conducted secondary research. Look at you, you researcher, you! Basically, secondary research is any research which you yourself did not conduct. But does it mean that it's second rate or second best? Absolutely not! I think that secondary research is by far the best place to start. Seeing what others have found out about your question gives you a baseline of what's going on. Then you can confirm or deny what you are finding by doing your own primary research. Although please keep in mind that there are many (many!) less-than-reputable sources of information. I'd suggest that you never just take the information you find as gospel. Especially if it's a bit of information upon which you will make some big decisions, be sure that you can verify the source and find similar conclusions in other source material.

One of the best and easiest tools for secondary research is an online search engine like Google. That little search bar can access billions of websites in milliseconds, and it will return troves of information. When I searched for "churches attracting new members," Google found about 16.5 million results in 0.47 seconds. Obviously, you are not going to go through them all, but if you start to go through the top results, you will see some patterns.

You can also search for data about the church in the denomination itself. The Episcopal Church has an incredible resource available on their website to "get to know" your congregation and diocese.[1] Research firms such as Barna, Pew, and Gallup are also great places for insights because they are regularly researching religious trends in the United States. Along the way you will discover other similar

---

1. You can find it at https://episcopalchurch.org/research-and-statistics.

sources. Google itself will provide you with search terms related to "churches attracting new members."[2] Don't worry if this is the first time you've heard of Barna, Pew, or Gallup. Type into the Google search bar, "Who studies the church in the U.S.?" and you'll see about 447 million results in 0.63 seconds, and right there on the first page are all three. If you just know where to start with a simple question, the path starts to show itself.

Not all the information you find will be specific to your context. That will come a little later when you start to analyze and verify the data. Imagine that you find an article that has an interesting data point for you, but you realize that it's from a nondenominational Evangelical group. You might be tempted to dismiss it because your church is very traditional and liturgical. Don't throw it out! Our Evangelical brothers and sisters have done a ton of research about reaching those who have no religious or church affiliation. We can certainly learn from that knowledge. For now, just gather data.

The downside of all of this data being so easily available is that, well, there's tons of it and you'll probably spend at least a few hours or more sifting through it. But you don't have to do it all in one sitting and you certainly don't have to read it all. Skim over it and look for those little "Aha!" moments where you say to yourself, "Hmm, that's interesting." This is a good task that all members of the team can take on as a homework assignment and then share with the others what they found. All of you will find some of the same stuff for sure, but you will likely go down different rabbit holes and will find different insights. That's why you want a diverse team, so that others can find what you missed and so that you can share some things that they likely missed. Remember, the mindset is to be curious. Go explore.

Because Google keeps everything that has ever been on the internet (*everything!*), as you start to look at articles and research reports

---

2. As in, just search for "churches attracting new members" in Google.

and blog posts and whatever else you may find, notice the publication date. The more recent the data, the better, of course, but not everything will be from the last year. A good rule of thumb in doing these kinds of searches is to keep it within the last ten years. That said, if something you find to be a huge "Aha!" is fifteen or twenty years old, don't discard it. Think of it as a clue and then do more research to see if you can find current information that matches, or refutes, what you found.

At some point, you will want to take a breather. This is when you can start to analyze your findings. See if themes are showing up in the work. Are many recent articles related to one specific area? If you find a ton of material on "how the congregation greets people" and it's resonating with you, then the welcome process is a theme you'll want to explore further.

When you gather again with your team you will be excited about some of the things you are finding. That's great, but be open to the ideas of others and even if your insights are not used now, it doesn't mean they won't inform your work. Humility is a good virtue to have here. (Of course, I write this not from a vacuum but from experience. I have been the one who can't let go of a great insight. Sigh.) Just go in knowing that we are all learning and that in the end, we hope the Holy Spirit is guiding our work.

After you have all shared what insights you have found, it's time to start drawing some preliminary conclusions. The key word in that whole sentence is "preliminary." In all of this, we are trying to narrow down the information so that you can do more research. Think of this as a funnel. At the top, we are dropping in a lot of data. What we want to be able to do is to start to see what fits. Yes, that sounds a little vague, but this is one of those instances where your team, the themes, your context, and the Holy Spirit will play out. All of those things will lead to interesting conversations that will allow you to become more focused.

Imagine that in our question, "What if we intentionally sought out new members?" you found these insights:

- Hispanics in the U.S. still have an affinity toward religion.
- 10,000 baby boomers are retiring each day and will continue to do so for the next few years.
- Nones (people who select "no religious affiliation" in surveys) are surprisingly open to the Christian message of social justice.
- The population in your community is expected to grow by 20,000 young professionals in the 5-mile area around your church.
- People who are older are looking for meaning and deeper knowledge.

On the surface, they are all exciting opportunities. How do you choose what to focus on? This is where your context comes in to play. Regarding the Hispanic insight, does your congregation already have some Hispanic members? Does your priest speak good enough Spanish to offer ministry in that language? Regarding the Nones, does your church already have a social justice program? Is the church active in the community? If the population is about to grow with young professionals, do you have active programs for children? Is your church equipped to handle kids? When it comes to baby boomers, are they in your community? Are more people retiring to your community or away from it? Since we already have an insight related to older folks wanting to find meaning, how can knowing that inform what you're seeing here?

You see? In all of these, it's your context that will start to allow you to make some decisions and move the project along. You might decide that since you don't have a priest who speaks Spanish and no real connections to the Hispanic community, that would take too much. Also, your church is not known for social justice work. And you don't have the resources to redo the children's area and really don't have much of a children's ministry. Yes, all of these are possible options for the congregation, but are they viable? Being able to be honest about who you are as a congregation will clear the way for the more viable options. In this case, the second and last insights are related and the group feels that they represent the lower-hanging fruit of opportunity for new members. After all, the adult forums that the church has are well attended by members and might be of interest to those seeking meaning in life. Thus, the preliminary conclusion is that yes, you can intentionally reach out to new members, and reaching out to the retiring baby boomers seems like a good opportunity for you.

Here's how to conduct secondary research:

1. Define your goals and context—because there's so much out there, you want to be focused or you'll get lost.
2. Frame your research—this is where you develop your design question. But still be open to the possibility (likelihood!) that it will evolve and change. It's just a place to start.
3. Select and retrieve data—this is where you start the digging. Google is a great place. Explore! Remember the ten-year rule.
4. Proceed with analysis—at this point you need to start trying to make sense of what you are seeing. Identify the themes.
5. Compare findings—when the team gathers again, notice what you each are finding. All are valid at this point in the process, so be open to what you are hearing. Also, don't be too invested in what you have found.
6. Draw some preliminary conclusions—from the insights and your context, what is the best opportunity?

Observation

Now that we have some insights based on secondary research, we begin the process of confirmation. We want to confirm two things: first, that the secondary research matches the reality. And second, that our preliminary conclusions about the data and our church are correct as well.

When we observe, we are trying to see if any of the research data is evident to the eye. I like to think of this like one of those National Geographic documentaries. "And now, we see the baby boomers in their natural habitat," says the deep-voiced announcer. Another way of thinking about this is that you are a detective on a stakeout. You're looking at normal, everyday situations with a curious eye. Especially, you want to be able to confirm or prove wrong what you have found in your research so far. As you observe you might also discover new insights. "The person did this *and* they also did that, which was very interesting."

Start by defining the area you want to observe. We have decided that we want to reach out to baby boomers and their search for meaning. What we are doing is to see whether the reality around us matches what we have found in the research.

To define the area, think like the object of your observation might think. (I told you it was like being a detective!) Ask yourself, if I were a baby boomer and wanted more meaning, where might I find it? Some activities that come to mind might be volunteering, yoga, tai chi, adult education classes at the local college, maybe even a bookstore or library. Choose one to start with: volunteering. You'll then find some of the more popular places where people volunteer and go check it out. Maybe it's the local animal shelter or the food bank. You have just defined your area to observe.

Let's go with volunteering at the local food bank. At first, you just want to observe. Are baby boomers volunteering in larger numbers? Check out the volunteers and compare the ages and who they are. You could have just as easily spent some time at the Barnes & Noble bookstore and see where the baby boomers go when they shop there.

The second step is to select your participants thoughtfully, to make sure that they do match what you are looking for in the data. It's very easy to get distracted and want to go down other rabbit holes. This is not the time for that. You can always study that another time. In this case, you want to observe baby boomers for their behavior.

You now want to make sure that you carefully observe. This sounds odd since that's literally why you're there. What I mean is that you want to make sure that you are not just looking for them to confirm what you already think and believe. That is called confirmation bias. So, challenge your assumptions. Assume you want to prove yourself wrong. And remember that you really want to look for insights here too, because they can show you something in their behavior you didn't expect.

Maybe you realize that the volunteers in your demographic showed up early and stayed late beyond the time when others left, and that they are chatting up with others a lot. You might determine from this that perhaps the meaning is found not so much in the act of volunteering, but in the relationships they have with other people *while* they are volunteering. That's a new insight and one you can later check out.

Please, make sure that you are capturing your data. I find that having a notebook for journaling keeps it all in one place. This is a great time to record your own field notes. ("Day 42 . . . the baby boomers are social and fun!") Write down insights or questions that arise so that you can do more research later. If something catches your eye, you can even take a picture, but don't take photos of people without their express permission.

If you are not the type to go out and observe in person because that's not your style or you feel it's invading privacy, no worries. You can ask people to send YOU pictures! Ask your Facebook friends of a certain age to take a picture of their bookshelf or the last few books they have read and send it to you privately. You'll glean many insights from what they are reading and other items, and you'll feel comfortable knowing that they sent it to you. Let those who are more extroverted observe in person.

Once you have your data, gather the team and report back. It is in the moments when we share that we are starting to look critically at our data to see what is being confirmed, what is not, and whether you have new insights. If you do have new insights, then you can do some secondary research to see what you find. (Finally, secondary research would be second!)

Tips for better observation

1. Look for things that prompt behavior—what happened that caused someone to do something?
2. Look for adaptations—we all are used to adapting things that were meant to work for one thing to work as something else (life hacks to make things work better). For example, if you see someone stepping on a chair to reach up it means that there's not a ladder handy and that the item might be stored in the wrong spot.
3. Look for what people care about—by what they say, or the shirts they wear, or even bumper stickers, people can be very revealing.
4. Look for body language that expresses emotion—you don't need to be a psychologist to know what crossed arms or a frown means.
5. Look for patterns—be on the lookout for usual objects or routines. And if more than one person is doing it, there's likely a "there" there. A classic example of this is a new trail that is marked in the grass. Could it be because many people keep trying to avoid something in their path?
6. Look for the unexpected—look for anything out of place that might point to a need of those you are observing.

All along the way, remember that you are looking to match what you have found in the secondary research earlier. Is it true for your context? Maybe it is not. This is why you are observing. While you do, start thinking of opportunities that may be present.

You may also want to observe your own congregation. Does it match what you are finding out about your neighborhood? If not, is that an opportunity? If you are starting to see opportunities, are you in a position to take advantage of them?

Your congregation is exploring attracting newly retired folks who are looking for meaning, and you have discovered that socializing is a large part of what's involved. What are some of the opportunities you see? I read recently that salons (the deep-thinking kind, not the hair and nails kind) were making a comeback. Or maybe a nearby university has a good religious studies department. I have always thought that having a serious discussion about theodicy (how a good and all-loving God allows bad things to happen) would lead even non-religious folks to show up. This is especially potent for the progressive church, where we can ask questions even though we know we don't have satisfactory answers for them. As long as the opportunities we find have a social element to them, we'll be on course with the insights we found.

Even as we are starting to analyze and see some opportunities, there are still more insights we can find.

How to observe

1. Define area to observe—you have to know what you are observing.
2. Select participants thoughtfully—make sure that you are observing those that will yield some data and insights.
3. Carefully observe—remember, look to confirm or deny what you think you know. And look for new insights!
4. Capture data—you don't want to forget stuff, so take field notes and pictures when you can (if you feel comfortable).
5. Share back to the team—it's in the sharing back when the data starts to make sense.

Conversation

In design thinking, this method is called "interviewing." I love interviewing people. A friend reminded me that the etymology of "interview" comes from the French meaning to "glimpse at" whereas that for "conversation" is "to live among." Talk about an insight! When God wanted to get close to us, God sent Jesus to live among us. That's why we found a more appropriate name for our purposes.

Our mindset during the insights period is being curious. People love it when you are curious about them. The whole point of these conversations is about going deeper in what you are finding and especially doing so in your own context.

There are three steps to conducting a good structured conversation: plan, conduct, and share. Throughout, it is important to practice deep listening. Have you ever been in a conversation when you've asked a question and then while the other person is speaking, instead of listening, you are thinking of the great quip you will now say that will slay them all with laughter and show everyone just how smart you are? Really? Just me? It is rare that we actually pay full attention to the person speaking to us and then take a beat to think and then respond. When we are engaged in deep listening, we take the time to really listen to the other person to make sure that we hear and understand what they are saying. To keep myself in the deep listening mode during the formal conversations I conduct, I wait until the other person is completely finished speaking and then repeat back what I heard them say before I go to the next question. "Fascinating, so you are saying that for you, the sermon is the crux of the service. How would you say that influences your . . . ?" Doing this keeps me listening deeply since I have to repeat it. It also lets them know that I am really listening and caring about what they are saying. And it allows me to ask better questions because they are coming from what the person is saying.

Planning the conversation

Conversations will give you more insights, to help you learn more about what you're exploring. Be intentional, make sure that your conversations match where you are headed. You may want to have a conversation with some of the volunteers or someone who signed up for a class at the nearby college. It's easier than you think to get people to talk with you. You can stand outside the classroom and then ask them on the way out if they have fifteen minutes to chat about their experience. It's amazing how many people will talk to someone with a clipboard! Or the next time that you volunteer, invite one of your fellow volunteers to coffee to chat about their experience. Just make sure that they are in the correct demographic for your insights. These do not need to be strangers, by the way. I once put out a call to friends on Facebook to chat with young people about their church experience. Friends connected me with people they knew and I did some video conference conversations.

There is no "perfect" number of people you should talk to, though you'll want enough to get some variety and find some surprises. Somewhere in the range of five to ten conversations is a good number. You can take a short break and see what more you might need or if you have enough.

Once you have your subjects and think you know how to get to them, you want to prepare eight to ten questions that will satisfy your curiosity about what you are exploring. You can be as direct as "Tell me what brings meaning to your life." You want to get to know these individuals and their experiences.

The best questions are open-ended and cannot be answered with a simple yes or no. Think of questions that invite the person to tell you a story. A great prompt is always "Tell me about your typical day," because they will give you details that might become insights to follow up on. Telling you about their day allows you to see the decisions they

make and will be less likely to be what they think you want to hear. If
you ask someone whether they pray, they might say yes, but it may be
more of an aspirational statement than a truth. If you ask them to tell
you about their day and they mention the time they took for prayer,
that's a real answer.

Being able to see people's decision points is also very exciting as
a researcher. Once, I was trying to figure out why someone who had
a relationship with a church was only going every four weeks or so. It
surprised me, because she really enjoyed it when she was there. When
I asked her to "describe a typical Sunday," I could see that as a parent
she made tons of decisions throughout the day. And even if she had
the best of intentions about going to church, there were school projects to complete or kids' activities to attend. In those decisions were
more insights!

Rather than record a conversation, I find it's best to take notes
during the conversation, or have two members of the team present so
one takes notes while the other runs the meeting. (Side note: if you
are having a conversation with anyone younger than eighteen, make
sure that you have the parent's or guardian's permission and have been
trained in safe church practices. Further, following safe church practices, we at TryTank have a rule that if we are having a conversation
with a youth, we always have at least two adults present. Hopefully,
everyone on your team has had safe church training, as it is applicable
to how we conduct ourselves with people of any age.)

As you plan your conversation, it is important to keep in mind
consent and power dynamics. You want to make sure that at the start
of the conversation you cover consent, so it makes sense to make yourself a note of this at the top in the preparation notes. You want to
make it clear to the person you are chatting with that they are in
charge and that they can end the conversation at any time and that
they can ask that any part of it be completely anonymous. Make it
clear that you will respect that decision. Be sure that you are aware
of any power dynamics that may be involved. Does the person work

for someone the convener knows (and maybe that's how you found them)? Or maybe the interviewer is an older adult and the interviewee a younger person? It doesn't mean that you can't conduct this step if power differentials exist. Being aware of them allows you to work with or around them, or to find another person from the team to have the conversation.

Conducting the conversation

When you are conducting a conversation, keep in mind that they will all be different; in length, in content, and in what you find. And you have to be in the moment for it. So, for example, if you are having a short on-the-street chat, you will be in a different place mentally than if you go grab a cup of coffee with the person.

Remember to begin with explaining what it is that you are exploring: "We are trying to see how people find meaning in their life." Let them in on what you are seeking so that they will know how they can narrow their responses. Also, remember to be clear about the consent and that they can request anonymity. And ask them if they have any questions for you before you start.

As you start, you want to make sure that you are out of "survey" mode. You are not asking them to select from among five choices. You want to have a conversation guided by the eight to ten questions you have. Be open to surprises from the person. It is possible that they say something, and you say to yourself, "Hmmm, that's interesting." That's an insight! Follow that rabbit! Even if you only get to three of the ten questions on your question sheet, you could easily find new insights that will be very influential to your work.

Once I was having a fifteen-minute phone conversation with a seventysomething about their experience of watching church services digitally during the COVID pandemic. He was telling me about his day, and he said—almost in passing—something about digital church being "a good Plan B" to have. My ears perked up and I immediately asked about that. "Can you tell me more about what you mean by Plan B?" I asked. He then told me about mobility issues that someone his age has and how, sometimes he'll get up on a Sunday morning in unexpected pain. Before digital church, he'd have to either miss church and his social time there or go while in pain, which was not fun for him (or those around him). But now he could at least still partake in the sacred moment from home. I did some more research on the mobility issues and it turns out that a really large number of folks over sixty-five have mobility problems. I had no idea! And I never would have known if I had just stayed with my set questions and not followed my hunch.

Whatever you do, don't let your conversation plan keep you from going to unexpected places that arise. Follow those threads and ask why. As you design the conversation, make sure that you have put some purposeful "show me" moments when someone can take you into their life. Those are the meatier answers that you want.

On your side, remember to listen deeply and to be in conversation with them. During the conversation, take "headline" notes. In other words, write down something that you can fill in more details about once the conversation is over but be sure you get to this soon; you don't want to forget stuff or get your answers mixed up with another person you spoke with at another time.

Tips for a fruitful conversation

- Be sure to ask open-ended questions. If the question can be answered with yes, no, or maybe, it is not an open-ended question. Remember that this is a conversation rather than a survey. Ask how, when, or tell me about; ask "Why do you think that is?" Since it's a conversation, follow-up questions should be natural as they would be in chatting with a friend.
- Be sure to get specific examples rather than generalities. Ask for "show me" moments of something general they say. In fact, ask

for permission: "What you just said is fascinating; would you mind sharing an example from your own life about that?" If you deepen the connection, you can't go wrong!

- You want to start broad and finish deep. You want to get to know them and then get to the topics of interest. Be on the lookout for their emotions and feelings.

- Build rapport with the person. Be aware of your body language and facial expression. Feel sincere interest in them. In many ways, your tone matters as much as the questions. Remember to give all your attention to the person.

- Be sure to mind the gap. In your listening make sure that what they do, say, think, and feel all match. Look for the inconsistencies and build on that in a nonjudgmental, curious way. "I noticed you said X but you did Y, can tell me why you think that might be the case?"

Another approach to conversation is called the "Five Whys" method and it comes from the business world. The theory is that if you ask someone "Why?" five times, you will get to the core of what they mean. Let's say you ask me "Hey, Lorenzo, why do you go to church?" That's one why.

"Because I have always gone to church on Sunday?" I say.

"And why have you always gone to church on Sunday?" you say, deploying your second why.

I think and then say, "I guess because that's what we did with my mom every Sunday and it became part of my life."

Then you'd ask, "And why did your mom take you to church on Sundays?" using your third why.

"So that we would have a better relationship with Jesus."

"And why did she want you to have a better relationship with Jesus?" Fourth why.

"I guess because our life is better with Jesus in it."

"And why is your life better with Jesus in it?" Fifth why.

"Because he shows us how to live and teaches us about God."

So, in just five questions, we have gone from "because I always do" to "I go to church because I want Jesus to teach me how to live a better life and know about God." And you can see that the two are related, one is just a more thoughtful and intentional answer. Most of the time, we do things and we don't even know why we do it. An insight from this conversation might be that, since I am still going to this particular church, it is doing a good job of teaching me about how Jesus wants us to live our lives in God.

This method should only be a back-up plan for you since it's not as much an open conversation, but, if you get stuck, it's a way to move from there.

Sharing back to the team

It's important to share back with the team because you are likely to find even more insights as you retell the story and get others to ask you questions. And as you listen to what they report back, you will have questions for them. Their telling of their experiences might also lead you to see something in your conversation that you hadn't thought about but now makes sense in light of others saying they heard something. You will start to see themes. Are your earlier findings being supported by the evidence? What new insights did you all learn?

You may have a question asked of you that you simply didn't think to ask during the conversation. That's okay. You are allowed to call the person back and ask them about one thing you didn't ask or forgot to ask. Since they are being helpful, they will generally have no problem answering a question for you.

As you would have had conversations with people who have recently retired to get a glimpse at their lives, some will be people who are not involved in a church. Maybe you have discovered that they are reading nonfiction and watching documentaries. In learning about their lives, you might also learn that they have some deep doubtful questions about the Bible. These are good insights that we can use as we move along the process.

At this point, you might feel emboldened by what you are finding out and want to rush out and create a new ministry to get ALL of the recently retired folk to rush to your church. Good for you for finding the enthusiasm that this can bring! But there is more we can learn and a process to follow.

Empathy Experiences

The next method we'll explore for gaining insights is the empathy experience. In this context, empathy refers to our Christian intuitive ability to identify with another person's inner being. You do this by putting yourself in someone else's situation as best you can. It's the old "Walk a mile in someone else's shoes." It's intentionally trying to imagine what someone else's day is like to see how they live it and make decisions.

Keep in mind that there's a reason these four methods are in the order in which I have presented them here. It'd be pretty hard to try to have empathy with a group of people you have not identified, observed, and had a conversation to get to know. But now that you do have that bit of background it is easier to do this.

A great example of this is the "Plan B" conversation I mentioned just a moment ago. Once I realized (have gained an insight) that for a certain number of people, mobility is an issue, then I can imagine a bit better what their days are like, and especially how that impacts their ability to participate at church.

But there's something else. The data allows you to really imagine their daily life. This will give you new insights to explore. Also, when you do this you're experiencing some of what they experience first-hand, and this gives you an emotional connection. These are the best kinds of insights to gain since we make many of our decisions based on emotions.

An empathy experience also allows you to go beyond assumptions you didn't even know you had. When you turn the key to your car, you just assume that it will turn on, right? Well, for many people who drive older cars because that's what they can afford, sometimes turning the key is a little like spinning a prize wheel with a chance (maybe a good chance) that it will not turn on today. That assumption we take for granted is a cause for stress every morning as they want to go to work.

These empathy experiences also give us more than just insights and more knowledge. Empathy experiences allow you to feel the emotion. When I wanted to feel what it must be like to have my mobility be a totally random thing I could not control, I created an empathy experience. Around Mother's Day I wanted to spend some time with my mom on the phone. I really wanted to do this. It was important to me, like what going to church feels like for a single senior in our community. But to really feel the randomness that they sometimes feel when they wake up and are in so much pain they can't carry out their plans, I decided that I would leave calling my mom up to chance. I asked Google to generate a random number between 1 and 1 million. If it was an even number, I could call my mom. If it was an odd number, I would not be able to do so. Something I really wanted to do was left totally to chance. Then I hit enter. The resulting number was odd. I could not call my mom. It was like a punch to my stomach. And for that moment, I had a much better understanding of what it felt like to be prevented from doing something by random chance. I ended the empathy experience right then and there. My lesson was learned, and why should my mom suffer for my experiment?

If this sounds familiar, it is because empathy has a lot to do with being in relationship with people, and the church is about relationship with God and with each other.

Creating empathy experiences are best done as a team. By now, all of the team members have themselves been involved in the process. They have read information, observed, and had conversations. Best of all, they have been part of the sharing times as a team. So, all of you bring different perspectives you have gleaned along the way. These are all very important to creating authentic empathy experiences.

How to conduct an empathy experience

1. *Plan your experience:* This is not a random thing that will give you insights. To be effective, you need to be quite intentional about what you are seeking to learn. Take some time to consider the people you want to better understand. To better understand newly retired seniors who are looking for meaning, what needs more clarity? From what I have learned, what's something calling for a deeper, more emotional dive? One way to get there is to come up with five different answers to this question: What does it feel like to _____?

   For our retired seniors, we might ask:

   What does it feel like to not have to go to work every day?
   What does it feel like to get to reinvent yourself as a retiree?
   What does it feel like to consider what life has been all about?

   Note that these are all deep questions. These are not about superficial things. They will give you a new perspective on their lives.

2. *Brainstorm ideas:* Once you have a direction based on your questions, it's time to come up with experience ideas. As a team, brainstorm possible ideas that might give you the emotional insights you are seeking. You will want to come up with five to ten ideas. Take your time with this part. Really think them through. You'll have to be creative. These are emotional at the core.

Since I could not just come up with a way to give myself a mobility issue by random chance, I had to look at what I was trying to really get at: How can I randomly take away something I really wanted to do?

3. *Design it:* Now that you have a list of ideas, it's time to choose one. In looking them over, does one speak more to the group than the others? At the same time, your choice may be predicated on what you can actually accomplish because of time or resources. Next, you will want to design it in more detail by answering the following questions: What will you do? How will you do it? What props or tools do you need? Whose help will you need?

4. *Run it:* It's the moment, run the experience. It may be a very short experience. More likely than not, it will be considerably shorter than the time it took to think about it and then think about how to do it. For me it was as simple as going to Google and asking for a random number. Lot of time thinking; less than a minute to execute it. But, again, the learning was amazing.

5. *Share back:* The debrief is as important as ever here. The diversity of views will allow you to see the results of the experience from various vantage points. If you had a falling out with your mom and you haven't called her for the last ten Mother's Days, then randomly being told you can't call her was no big loss, right? It is in the sharing that the insights will become most clear.

This once more makes the case for being extra careful about picking your team. You want to make sure that all who are a part of this are curious people who want this process to work. One negative person on the team can significantly skew the outcomes.

Our empathy experience example

Based on the questions we came up with let's pick the first one: What does it feel like to not have to go to work every day? This question really has to do with meaning. I think that many of us find our purpose—our meaning—in what we do for a living. This is particularly true in the United States. So, what does it mean to no longer have the sense of who we are?

- We might consider what a typical day looks like to see where meaning can be found.
- We could try to come up with activities that can now have more meaning than before.
- We could actively look for meaningful opportunities in the community.

We'll choose looking for meaningful things to do or get involved with in the community. To design it, we will not plan anything on Saturday and instead, we will wake up and actively seek something meaningful to do. Do you Google that? Do you look in the paper? Can you find a thing to volunteer for at the last moment? Will they even take you if you haven't been vetted? This requires some thinking and creativity but it's not that hard and as a team, it's totally doable.

In all of this, you have been gathering the ingredients and putting them into a stew. It will take some time for all of the flavors to come together to make the meal. That's not only okay, but expected! You will see some connections only after you have had more conversations or other parts of the process.

Other Methods

The four methods that we generally use for our work are by no means an exhaustive list of the methods you may employ. In "Design Thinking:

Process and Methods" by Robert Curedale, you can find a list of seventy-six methods of "discovery" (his word for insights). This book is primarily concerned with how to use design thinking in the church and, specifically, the framework that TryTank uses. Our methods are about getting to know people more holistically. We are not looking to create a product. We are seeking to enter into relationships with people so that they can get to know and (hopefully!) follow Jesus of Nazareth and his redeeming message of God's love for the world. I encourage you to find the methods that work best for you and your context.

Sidebar: Getting Buy-In

The process of getting buy-in along the way breaks down into three steps that provide convenient points to share back with the leadership of the church, and by leadership, I mean the altar guild who we all know holds the power.

Why to get buy-in is fairly simple: none of us like to be surprised and feel left out. If while being informed, we can make people feel that they are being heard, that's golden! The more people feel involved along the way, the more they are likely to have buy-in, or at least not try to impede the work.

- As the process is starting and you want to recruit team members, put the word out to the parish and see who's interested. Explain to as many people in the congregation as you can what you will be doing and what the goal is. Ask for feedback about the initial design question you may have.
- After each of the three steps (insights, ideas, trying), let folks know how the work is going and what you are finding through an insert in the bulletin or a talk at the Sunday forum. Put your learnings up on the website.

- As you are designing ideas, seek out the more vocal members of the congregation and have coffee with them. Tell them what's going on. Get their thoughts on it as well.

When you get feedback along the way, when the time comes to launch something, the congregation will feel more invested in the work you have been doing and will be rooting for you. Being informed and being heard are two keys to getting people to come aboard.

I have been in ministry enough to know that there will always be detractors from the work. That's just life. Whenever I give a presentation about the work of TryTank, the audience usually breaks down into thirds:

- One-third are thinking "Oh, aren't you cute with your experiments and stuff! You keep doing that and we'll keep doing our stuff."
- One-third are thinking "Hmmm . . . I don't know who you are, but you might be the devil and I'll have to protect the church . . . might have to stop you at some point."
- And one-third are thinking "I'm in! Sign me up! How can we do this too?"

I tend to just focus on the last third, the supporters. If you have detractors, focus on the ones who realize that God is always making all things new again. They will hold you up if things get tough and will very likely be your defenders as well.

4 ↻→

STEP TWO:
Developing Ideas

The mindset for this step: Be playful.

Now that you have explored and gained some insights, what's next? It's time to take those ideas and start to turn them into possible things to try. Before we move on, we invite God's presence and participation.

Begin with Prayer

In doing this work, it's essential to remember that it's for the greater glory of God, to spread the good news of Jesus. I have noticed that if we are not intentional in reminding ourselves to pray, it's easily skipped. Sometimes we get so excited by the work that we just want to jump right on in to do it. That's great! And please, take the time to begin with prayer.

This being holy work is especially palpable in the second step. We can invite the Holy Spirit to be with us and inspire our work. I believe that the Holy Spirit is the creative muse the church has always had and will always need. So, invite the Divine to open our minds to new possibilities we may not think of on our own.

You do not have to be the best at extemporaneous prayer. Use the Book of Common Prayer, your denomination's own prayer book, or simply open your mind and heart and say the Lord's Prayer. That's enough for what we want, which is to orient ourselves to God so that we can trust that God is with us in this process. Now that we are in a God-centered space, let's get to work.

Shifting Our Question

What we want to do next is to shift our design question. Now that we have those insights that give us a clearer direction, we are ready to go from "What if . . . ?" to "How might we . . . ?" This shift takes us from an inquiry to inform our research to an action step. It will actually position your mind to think differently about the question, so it's no longer about finding out more but about making something happen. This is how you can discover new ways to try and, in some cases, true innovation. I love this shift!

At TryTank, we have a bias toward action, but then again, doesn't God? Think about it. During the sermon on the mount, Jesus shows that God prefers it when we do something: "Ask, and you will receive. Search, and you will find. Knock, and the door will be opened to you. For everyone who asks, receives. Whoever seeks, finds. And to everyone who knocks, the door is opened" (Matt. 7:7–8).

Once, someone asked, "Can't we just start at the second step? Wouldn't we get to the same place if we had begun with "How might we seek out new members?" (They probably are the type of person that begins a book by reading the ending!) The short answer is that of course you can, BUT it is not the same.

When you begin with "How might we . . . ?" you don't have data to inform your answer to the question. It will be much less specific and doesn't take advantage of opportunities in your own neighborhood.

That is the beauty of the insights step. Those insights will inform the answers to the 'How might we . . . ?' question you are now ready to ask. We have gone from "What if we intentionally sought out new members?" to a new, more specific question based on our insights: "How might we reach newly retired folks with something that gives them a sense of meaning?" The design question is not etched in stone. It might still evolve more, but it is specific enough to allow us to start getting some good ideas.

How to Come up with Ideas

Here are four methods we regularly use at TryTank to come up with ideas. Keep in mind that the more ideas you have, the further out of the box you are likely to go. The mindset for this step is to be playful. Be more like a kid and less like an adult. This also means that for right now, at this stage, there are no bad ideas. Take them all in. Leave the judgments for later when that time comes.

The mash-up

A mash-up is when you take two things and, well, mash them into a new thing. You've probably heard of this being done in music, when they take a sample of one song and put it into a new song, or in cooking when two foods are combined into a new fusion dish. If you have ever taken a creative writing course, you may have seen the exercise where you take something from column A (an occupation, for example) and mash it with something from column B (a scenario), which is how you end up with a prompt for a new story (a priest who inherits a billion dollars!). You take things that might normally not go together to create new things.

The concept is pretty much the same for our purposes. The key factor to consider when doing a mash-up is that two totally unrelated sets of data work best to produce truly unique new ideas. So, don't be limited by thinking that you need to look at things that only or normally go with church. You can also look at two categories that have some sort of relationship with each other. The process works the same. In theory, your insights will start to provide you with some of the categories to consider.

1. *Reframe the question:* Make sure that you have reframed your question to something that seeks specific actions. Remember, it's now "How might we . . . ?"

2. *Choose the categories:* Pick two unrelated categories that can give you new ideas. By unrelated, I don't mean oil and water, but rather things that normally would not be thought about together. As to *how* unrelated the categories, that is something you have to feel. You'll know when something is too unrelated for what we are seeking. Trust your instincts. Draw a line down the middle of a sheet of paper. At the top of one column, write in one category. On the other column, put the name of the other category.

3. *Generate elements:* Now that you have your categories, list as many elements for each that you can. You want to have a minimum number of about ten to actually get the creative juices flowing. But if you're in the flow and have more than ten, then all the better. Go for as many as you can. This is another great reason that a team is better than individuals. You will always get more ideas because multiple brains are working on it and we all see things a little differently.

4. *Mash them up:* This is the fun, creative part. Go wild! Remember that at this point there are no bad ideas; there are only ideas that haven't been expressed. If you are looking at the elements and feel stuck, then just go down the lists and start to mash them up one by one. Take the first element from column A and just go down the whole of the elements from column B. And keep going.

Here's what it might look like:

CATEGORY A   CATEGORY B

_____   _____

_____   _____

_____   _____

_____   _____

_____   _____

_____   _____

For our design question, "How might we reach newly retired folks with something that gives them a sense of meaning?" our categories are (A) things to do with free time and (B) things that give meaning.

(A) FREE TIME	(B) MEANING
Read	Praying
Paint	Meditating
Work out	Serving
Travel	Journaling
Volunteer	Learning
Side gig	Poetry
Movies	Listening to music
Go to the library	Being in nature
Take a class	Talking with a friend
New hobby	Donating money

What are the resulting mash-up ideas? Reading and being in nature (a book club that meets at the national park?); taking a class and poetry (offering a poetry workshop?); movies and learning (a series of documentaries to learn about new things?).

These two categories are not too far apart from each other (and our topic). But what if we really wanted to get creative? Let's try this again, but instead of things to do with free time, let's list elements of what makes a good luxury hotel and see what we come up with.

(A) MEANING	(B) LUXURY HOTEL
Praying	Elegant design
Meditating	Lots of flowers
Serving	High thread-count sheets
Journaling	Friendly staff
Learning	Room service
Poetry	Mini bar
Listening to music	Great food
Being in nature	Live piano music
Talking with a friend	Gift shop
Donating money	Spacious room

So, the mash-ups here might be: journaling and great food (a dinner club that journals together?); donating money and a gift shop (running a Christmas gift shop to raise money for a cause?); meditating and room service (a meditation retreat at a nice place where all the practical needs are taken care of by others?). This technique is fun and produces interesting ideas.

Other people's shoes

In this method of coming up with ideas, what you want to do is get as many shoes from other people and then wear them for a week. (Beat.) Just kidding! I sure hope you're reading the whole section before going and doing things.

"Walking in someone else's shoes" is a way to really understand them. This method is related to the empathy experience we looked at in the insights phase. The "other people" whose shoes we are going to walk in are these retired folks who are looking for meaning. For me, it actually helps to give them a name and a back story since it makes it more real. So, let me introduce you to Wendy, a recently retired real estate lawyer who now lives in our community. She's sixty-seven, married to Robert, and they live alone. They have two kids and six grandkids who all live out of state. They also have a dog named Lucy. They are middle class. Like most new retirees, they are looking for meaning in life. As we think through a day in their shoes, I will also list possible ideas in parentheses in order to show you how the ideas start to present themselves.

When Wendy gets up, she eases into the day by making coffee while listening to some soft music in the background. (A podcast of soft music with short inspirational messages?) She then reads the paper while drinking her coffee. (A weekly "exploring theology" column in the paper?) After the paper she'll do some yoga for exercise and to clear her mind. (Maybe team with a local instructor and record some Christian yoga sessions to have available for people to view online?) She'll then have breakfast, shower, and get dressed for the day. At mid-morning, she will head out in her car to run some errands. In the car, she'll listen to a podcast of an advice call-in show she finds entertaining. (How about the church produces a fun and entertaining advice podcast about life with deep dives into subjects?) . . .

I could go on with the rest of the day, but you can see how we came up with four ideas before Wendy has even had lunch. When you do this with your team and are truly open to the work of the Holy Spirit, then you can easily come up with twenty ideas as you go through her day. Remember, no judging—yet!

None of the ideas mentioned here are earth-shattering innovations that no one had ever heard about; they are all things that are already part of Wendy's world. They have just been repurposed for the use of the church in the world.

If you are a visual person and not just an imaginative person, you can create a storyboard for the different points in the story of the day. A storyboard has just a few squares on a sheet of paper with some very simple drawings. You will be surprised how, for visual people, they are an amazing prompt to "see" the day and come up with ideas.

eStorm

An eStorm is like a brainstorm, but through email. For any introverts out there, this is right up your alley!

An actual brainstorm is better since when you are in person ideas can spring from other ideas, but an eStorm is not a poor substitute, either. It has its own merits. Doing it via email allows you to gather ideas from people all over the place, not just the ones you can gather in a room at the same time. It also allows you to reach more people, since you can send an email to a hundred people at the same time but there's no way you can run an effective brainstorm with that many people. Finally, inviting wide participation from people beyond your team is a great opportunity to continue to get buy-in from the congregation.

After you say a little prayer, keep the design question in mind. This will inform the rest of the steps.

1. *Start with the subject line:* In drafting the email, your subject line must be provocative in order to break through in a sea of so many other emails.

2. *Manage expectations:* Be clear that you're seeking just a few minutes of their time. People are busy. So, manage the expectation that this will be quick, and they will be helping you out. People love to help. Be sure to mention the deadlines you have set. I like to bold them and then make them a different color. It stands out more that way. Be sure to thank them!

3. *Present the challenge:* Be brief. Set up the challenge you are facing. Use your design question since it is now seeking specific actions in response. Be sure to provide an example of an idea you already have come up with to help them get into a playful mindset. The example also demonstrates that their response can be short and quick. Remember to thank them!

4. *Pictures work!* In your instructions, you can ask them to attach sketches or photos of their ideas if that helps. Rather than trying to describe something they may not be really able to explain

in writing, a picture really can be worth a thousand words! Have you thanked them yet?

5. *Follow up with a vote:* After you and the team get all of the ideas and you have selected the ones that seem to fit the challenge, then follow up with those who participated. Share with them the top three ideas you think solved the challenge and ask your participants which one they think is best. Once more, be sure to thank them for participating in this with you and the team.

What an eStorm looks like:

From: Lorenzo Lebrija <lorenzo@trytank.org>
Date: Friday, September 4, 2025 at 10:15 AM
To: YOU

Subject: Can I borrow 3.5 minutes?

Dear X,

I need your help and it'll take just three and a half minutes of your time.

As you probably know, I am on a committee at church trying to get new members. Woot! The work has been fun and after some research, we came up with a question: How might we reach newly retired folks with something that gives them a sense of meaning?

If you were trying to come up with just ONE idea to answer that question, what would it be? For example, I think the church should invite a professor from the university for a one-day deep dive into philosophy. This would bring folks from the neighborhood to our church where we can introduce them to what we do. What would be your idea? If you want to send a drawing or a picture to describe it, feel free to do so.

If you are thinking of an idea right now, just hit reply and send it my way. Those can be really good. If you need a little more time, then please take it. We are trying to get as many ideas back by September 9, 2025. We will then select a few and ask you to vote on the one you like best.

If you have any questions just let me know.

Thank you, thank you, thank you (!!) for your help with this.

Sincerely,
Lorenzo

You'll note that it's a short and simple email that manages expectations and asks for just a moment that's designed to get a good response from your friends, colleagues, and church members. Please DO NOT expect that everyone you send it to will respond. If you get 25 percent to respond, you are doing very well. That's the beauty of email; if you send it to a hundred people and get twenty-five of them back, that's twenty-five ideas and many might be new to you and the team. And if you have four people on your team and they all get twenty-five responses, you now have a hundred ideas to consider. It really is an eStorm of possibilities!

Brainstorming

Please don't jump over this section! Because brainstorming is something we are familiar with, we think we know how to do it and then don't get great results. Brainstorming is an incredibly potent tool because it can get you to a place where no individual could end up by themselves. There is something powerful when people hear a new idea that then triggers something in them and that leads them to a new idea; a new place. That's the power of a good brainstorming session. Check out the Sidebar on page 73 about the "The Adjacent Possible" for a quick look at why this is so!

1. *Get a leader:* Assign a group leader for the session. The leader's main job is to keep creative ideas flowing. They make sure that every person is participating and every idea gets heard and recorded. They also can keep the time. In a way, they are a cheerleader for creative ideas! The leader steps in when the rules are breached (especially the "There are no bad ideas" rule).
2. *Get the right number of people:* You'll need between four and seven people in the session. With fewer than that, there's the risk that stimulation will not flow. More than seven runs the risk that not everyone will be heard. If your core team is between four and seven, you're golden. Add a few more if you have fewer people or if you simply want more creative voices. Make sure that anyone you invite is someone who will contribute and who understands what it is you are trying to do. Update them on what the team has been up to and what your insights have been.
3. *The question:* Make clear what you are looking for in a brainstorming session. Put the design question on a flip chart so that it can be seen by all and so it guides the session. Make sure that everyone knows, understands, and is clear on what the question is really seeking. Talk it through briefly and allow people to ask questions.
4. *Know the rules:*

    -   There are no bad ideas! Be sure to defer judgment of ideas.
    -   There are no budget constraints and no boundaries in brainstorming!
    -   Encourage wild ideas; especially ideas that build on the ideas of others.
    -   If it helps, be visual. Sketch out the idea if it's easier than words. Act it out and have someone else help put it into words.
    -   Stay focused on the question. Repeat it out loud often. When in doubt, ask your "How might we . . ." question with the new idea as the answer. You'll see if it's gone off course.

- Keep it to one conversation at a time. Think of these as just headlines of the idea.
- Go for quantity. At this point in the process, quantity is much better than quality. More options will get you closer to the great idea.
- For the love of God, laugh! I firmly believe that creativity and laughter are related. This also helps to assure those who are more shy in the group that it's okay to put out an idea, even if it seems a bit crazy.

5. *Run the session:* A good brainstorming session will run between 15 and 45 minutes long. The best time is 30 minutes. The minimum number of ideas (in) should be the total of your session time (t) plus 5, or in = t + 5. So, if you are going for 30 minutes, you'll have no less than 35 ideas at the end of the session. Don't go over the allotted time and make sure you have the total ideas you set out to get. The best ideas will likely come toward the end when the pressure increases. I have seen this happen again and again.

   Make sure that either everyone has some Post-its for the ideas or that one person will jot them down on the flip chart. Start by taking turns with each person offering an idea. Then the free-flowing nature of the session will take over and ideas will come from all over. It may start slowly. The pressure of the time constraint and the minimum number of ideas will lead to ideas that are even further out of the box.

6. *Breathe:* You did it. Yay! Breathe for a second and take a little break to just be.

7. *Organize the ideas:* Cluster the ideas into related ideas. This is why having them on Post-its is nice since they are easy to move around. You might even be able to merge some of the ideas into a new, fuller idea.

A good brainstorming session can point out areas that make you once more say, "Hmm, that's interesting . . ." and then you can go and research more about what triggered that insight. Likewise, you might have an idea but it is dependent upon the answer to a question you hadn't asked. It is great when that happens because now you can go find out!

Good news. Your brainstorming is complete and now you have a list of ideas to move to the next step in the process. Do not make decisions on what to do about the ideas just yet. It's time to consider all of the ideas together from all of the idea-generating methods you used.

What Do We Do with All These Ideas?

Now that you have perhaps used a mash-up, spent time in someone else's shoes, conducted an eStorm and a brainstorm, it is time to start to narrow once more. Here's how you can do that.

Cluster

Group ideas together, merge as needed, and look for themes. It's perfectly fine if there are outlying ideas that don't fit into a cluster. Be generous when merging ideas. They don't have to have the exact same words; themes count, too. If one theme has a substantial number of ideas then your group may have more energy for that.

Discard some

Remember how we said that there are no bad ideas? Well, that's so all of the ideas will be considered in brainstorming, and this makes people feel comfortable in sharing and it's possible that a really crazy idea can trigger a new idea in someone that they otherwise would not have thought about. But now, it is time to put away the ideas that are simply not feasible. Be careful not to throw out ideas because they are hard. That's different from impossible or unreal. A way to do this is to make sure that you ALL agree that an idea is impossible or unreal.

Vote

Let's say that you are down to between ten and twenty ideas. As a team, vote for the three to five ideas that most resonate with you all. You have been on a journey together, so you are in a good position to do this. You know the insights you have gathered, you have been in conversations, so trust that God is in this with you as well. You may come back to some ideas in the future.

While doing this, think of your church, too. Who are the members? Might they make an otherwise impossible or unlikely idea possible? Remember how we listed an idea of running a weekly article in the local newspaper? What if someone in your congregation works at the local newspaper? That insight can make an unlikely idea more likely.

Moving to the next step

With three to five ideas, discuss as a team which are the one or two you want to take to the next step. Just because you're putting other ideas aside for now, it does not mean you won't ever come back to them.

To reach newly retired folks with something that gives them a sense of meaning, we generated these ideas:

- A deep-dive philosophy class from a university professor.
- A dinner club that journals together.
- Running a Christmas gift shop to raise money for the poor.
- A meditation retreat at a nice place where all the needs are taken care of by others.
- A podcast of soft music with short inspirational messages.
- A weekly "exploring theology" column in the paper.
- Recorded Christian yoga sessions for people to view.

- A weekly fun and entertaining advice podcast about life with deep dives into subjects.

And once we gathered to discuss these ideas in our own context, we decide that we will move these two to the next step:

- A weekly "exploring theology" column in the paper.
- A deep dive philosophy class from a university professor.

Great! It's time to move on to the third step, trying.

Sidebar: The Adjacent Possible

A few years ago, I read Steven Johnson's *Where Good Ideas Come From: The Natural History of Innovation*. It was the first time I heard the concept of "the adjacent possible" to describe how innovation happens. He painted a visual image to describe it that I still think about often:

Imagine that you are in a square, twenty-by-twenty-foot room. You are standing squarely in the middle of the room. On every one of the four walls around you there is a door directly in the middle of that wall.

The room you are in represents the reality you know and live right now. Each of the four doors represents a new reality that builds on the current reality. You can only go in incremental steps from one reality to the new reality that builds on where you came from. That's the adjacent possible.

Imagine that your reality (the first room) is a car in the 1950s. It's cool and faster than before, but because of the faster speed, now there are more accidents. It wasn't until 1959 that someone decided, "Hey, what if we put a belt in the car to keep us in our seat if there's an accident?" That's one of the doors in the first room. When that happened in 1959, we crossed from the first room to the seatbelt room. This new room became reality and there are now four new possible adjacent realities.

The first room is needed to make it to the next room. You could not develop seat belts for a car before there was a car, and one that went fast enough to cause deadly accidents. Innovation builds on itself. That is the adjacent possible. When Steve Jobs developed the iPod, he was building on the Walkman before it. (For you young ones, a Walkman was a portable cassette player. We were limited to traveling with just one cassette worth of songs, not every song ever recorded.)

While innovation generally builds on itself, there are times when visionaries show us what's possible. Leonardo Da Vinci drew a helicopter 420 years before one was actually built. He did not go to the adjacent room; he went into a whole different building. Thank God for those people. We need the visionaries! For the rest of us, we can find comfort that the natural process is that we go to the very next room, to the adjacent possible.

By the way, Jules Verne did not invent the submarine when he penned *Twenty Thousand Leagues Under the Sea* in 1870. British mathematician William Bourne drew the first submarine plans in 1578, and the first one was built by Dutch inventor Cornelis Drebbel in 1620. Verne's imagination gave us a version of the adjacent possible for submarines.

There is a benefit to NOT creating something 420 years before it's possible. We get to experience it! Da Vinci never got to see a helicopter or many of the other amazing things he sketched out in his books. We, on the other hand, in moving to the next room, can see what we dream of become real. In looking at the adjacent possible in our settings, we know we are moving forward by building on what we already have.

STEP THREE:
Trying

The mindset for this step: Be courageous.

Please take a moment now to see how far you have come. You have looked for insights and then sought out ideas. You have walked the walk and should be proud that you have made it here. Well done!

What does it mean to have a courageous mindset? In this work of trying new things, we are going to be scared that they won't work. It takes courage to say, "Let's just try it." This does not mean that you run toward danger or are not prepared for risk at all. It just means that we recognize that all of this involves a certain amount of anxiety. With God at the center, we go forward to try.

A Word about Enthusiasm

Years before seminary, I went to business school for my MBA. (Some would call that the anti-seminary, but I just point to law schools!) The final project for the program was a group presentation of a new business to actual venture capitalists who were looking to be tough on our ideas.

I didn't think our idea was the best ever. It was an ecotourism lodge in Costa Rica. Meh. I led the pitch. I was in the flow. I had their undivided attention. I was thinking, "Holy Toledo, maybe I was wrong, and this is the best idea and I just couldn't see the forest for the trees."

When it was over, I stood there, in the pit of the auditorium classroom at the university and waited for their comments and questions. After a pause, one of the venture capitalists addressed me. "You are going to be a millionaire!"

"It really is a good idea, isn't it?" I said, almost starting to see the forest.

"Oh, no," he responded. "Your idea is boring and will never work for many reasons. But the way you present, your enthusiasm—that's going to make you rich."

I discovered something that day—besides confirming that my gut instinct about the eco-business was right. I learned that enthusiasm is contagious. Launching something—anything—is hard, but your enthusiasm will make a huge difference. You can psych yourself up and bring others along with you. (And make sure that you listen to your gut. It's usually right.)

Tools for Trying

A Mission Canvas is basically a one-page business plan that allows you to look at nine important areas of consideration on one simple page. What we call Mission Canvas is an adaptation of the Lean Canvas[1] from the business world. Rather than spending weeks developing a long business plan that is dozens of pages that won't usually be read in

---

1. Mission Canvas is adapted from Lean Canvas (https://leanstack.com/lean-canvas) and is licensed under the Creative Commons Attribution-ShareAlike 3.0 Unported License. We have changed the headings and descriptions to reflect church *mission* rather than *business*.

full and will need to change when it meets reality, the Mission Canvas is quick and easy to adapt. You should be able to finish it in fifteen minutes. Each of the nine areas offers the opportunity to say, "Have we thought this part through?" This holistic approach lets you realize what you may still be missing and where you're really clear. It's also an incredible tool for sharing an idea with others and to continue to get buy-in from the congregation.

It works because it's easy to use. When you need to adapt it, it takes just a few minutes to change the canvas so that it's always the most up-to-date version. The Mission Canvas is really a working, living document.

This is what the Mission Canvas looks like:

(1) THE NEED	(3) STAKEHOLDERS	(4) ELEVATOR PITCH	(6) PARTNERS	(2) OUR SOLUTION
EXISTING ALTERNATIVES	(9) KEY METRICS		(5) PATH	
(8) EXPENSES		(7) FUNDING SOURCES		

Mission Canvas is adapted from Lean Canvas and is licensed under the Creative Commons Attribution-Share Alike 3.0 Un-ported License. We have changed the headings to reflect mission rather than business.

While you can download a PDF copy at www.MissionCanvas.org, please note it does NOT need to look like this. You can simply grab a blank sheet of paper, copy the headings, and go to town. It would defeat the purpose if a tool that is meant to make your life simpler actually became a block to getting it done. It's the content, not the layout that matters.

Basic Mission Canvas rules

1. *It takes 15 minutes:* To fill out the Mission Canvas should not take you more than 15 minutes. If it is taking you longer, you are probably overthinking it. I would recommend that it be written by one person and then the others can review and add while the whole team discusses what's on the Mission Canvas. If you try to do it as a team, it will take longer and the work will lose some of its punch.

2. *It's a suggested order:* The nine important areas covered by the Mission Canvas are in a particular order for a reason you will soon see. However, if you don't like the order, change it. This is meant to be a helpful tool, so make it your own. Likewise, if you don't like one of the section headings, change it to something that makes more sense in your context. While we are at it, the size of the blocks in the Mission Canvas are intentional. More space is given to the ones where more needs to be said, but don't be "boxed" into thinking you need to go a certain length! (See what I did there?) Just know that you have to think it through.

3. *It's okay to skip, but come back:* One of the best things that the Mission Canvas does is to walk you through all nine areas. But as you fill it out, it is possible (maybe even likely) that you will get to something you have not yet thought about. That is perfect! The Canvas is meant to show you the holes in the plan. So, skip the section for now and keep going. Then, do some

investigation and come back to fill in the missing information. You do not want to launch something without having filled in all parts of the plan.

4. *One canvas per idea:* Since the Mission Canvas is simple to fill out, use one per idea. By this point you are down to the best ideas from the process and this will help you look at the final ideas in a more holistic manner. Now you can decide which one to try!

The nine important areas

We will now turn to the nine important areas that the Mission Canvas covers in more detail. The clearer you can be in your mind about what the Mission Canvas seeks, the faster you will be able to fill it out.

We are filling out the mission canvas based on our design question: How might we reach newly retired folks with something that gives them a sense of meaning? For our example purposes, we will fill out the canvas as we progress, looking at the first of our two best ideas, the column in the paper. Remember that you will want to fill one out for each. I want you to see that the content is meant to be short and to the point. And while this will likely really hurt my college English professor, you don't even have to use full sentences or perfect grammar.

***Area #1** The need (plus existing alternatives):* List the core need that your idea is trying to meet. More likely than not this is directly related to your design question. This is not the need that caused the initial investigation (our church needs more members), but rather the need you identified in the community that the idea you are looking to try will fill (newly retired folks are looking for meaning). This is at the core of your solution. You also will want to list some of the other options that are currently meeting this need. In our case, you could list volunteering, reading, learning, and social events. We learned this in the first step, insights. Area 1 is complete, and that takes us to . . .

Area #2 *Our solution:* Here, list your proposed solution to the need you have identified. This is basically one of the results of the idea phase. Our solution is a weekly "exploring theology" column in the paper. The order is sequential: we identified the need and our solution. Now, we are ready for . . .

Area #3 *Stakeholders:* There are multiple stakeholders. First, there are beneficiaries, the newly retired folks. Who else will make decisions, or can influence decisions, about the idea? I bet that "vestry" will have some say. Since our idea is a newspaper column, the newspaper is a stakeholder since they could say yes or no to a free column, or they could offer to sell us some space. The writer is a stakeholder. We are figuring out who's involved in making this happen. Next, we need . . .

Area #4 *The elevator pitch:* In the list we just made for Area 3, there are folks who have not heard our idea yet. We want to be able to share it with them quickly and efficiently, making sure we're all on the same page when talking about it. In an elevator ride of under a minute or so, how would I pitch it to you? The core of your idea should be so crystal clear that just a few words will be enough. Building on our work, we say, "In order to reach newly retired folks who are seeking meaning to let them know about our church and what we have to offer, we want to publish a regular column exploring theology in the local paper." The pitch has our goal, our solution, and our beneficiaries. Simple is best. Now that we are clear, it's time for . . .

Area #5 *The path:* If the first four areas were a recap of what led us here, the next areas ask how we'll go forward. For our example, the path to the beneficiaries is the newspaper column itself. To use a different example, a new ministry to tutor kids, you would describe how to reach the kids. Would it be through the local schools? Is it through parents in the neighborhood? That's the path: how will you reach the beneficiaries. Moving on to . . .

Area #6 *Partners:* We in the church often overlook partners who can make our work easier, and miss opportunities that will strengthen and connect us. Here, the newspaper itself could be a partner. If a member of the congregation has an established relationship with the newspaper, they might want to partner in running the column. The writer is a partner. If we need to buy space to run the column, a local business could partner with the church in sponsoring the column. A local radio station might be a partner to promote the column, which convinces the newspaper to carry it since it's free publicity for them. Look at possible scenarios to determine possible partners. The underlying question is, "Who can help our new idea succeed?"

It's also important to ask, "Who is doing this already?" We may not need to invent everything if we can partner with someone who's already done work in this area. In most areas, the odds are good that someone near you already has done something that can help you out.

Area #7 *Funding sources:* Even if you change the order of the mission areas, I suggest you keep Areas 7 and 8 together, as they inform each other. When we dream up something new, one of the first questions we ask is "How much is this going to cost?" and we make a list of the expenses. Maybe it comes out to $3,000. Then we make a list of places we can get funds. This totals $2,000. I know what often happens next. Someone will say, "Well, we can't afford it, so, let's not do it." And a great idea comes to a premature death. By looking at the funding sources first, we are telling ourselves, "We have $2,000. How can we make this work for that amount?" Then we look at the expenses. This simple shift in the mindset can be huge in getting this done.

When looking at funding sources, count both cash and in-kind donations. And much like when you used to look for change to buy a treat from the ice cream truck, be sure to look between the cushions. In other words, think of all possible options. This might even be a good idea for a short brainstorm session. (Be sure to use the time + 5 rule from brainstorming!)

Where can we get funding for our idea of running a "theology explained" column? Since someone in the congregation works at the newspaper, we can explore the possibility of getting the column space donated. Alternatively, we can buy the space at a discount. Both the donated space and the discount are in-kind donations. To determine value, figure out how much the space would cost (we estimated $300 each time). If the column runs every two weeks for 12 weeks, that's a total of six times. The $300 times 6 totals $1,800. If the person who works at the paper thinks they can get a 50 percent employee discount, then the discount value is $900.

Then consider what can be raised from individuals or from fundraising efforts. Can each member of the four-person team commit to raising $500 from their friends, family, and events? Through Facebook and the internet, you can now reach out to friends all over. (And when you do this, you are also telling the world that your faith, your church is important to you. You know what we call that? Evangelizing!)

This is also a good time to consider getting even more buy-in, this time in a literal sense from the other members of the vestry and the rest of the congregation. Enthusiasm is contagious: if people hear you talk about your idea, they will get excited and want to help out. Between your fundraising prowess and what the congregation can set aside, you can raise up to $2,500. Well done! Now let's look at how to make it happen for that amount or less!

Area #8 *Expenses:* Just because you have access to the money you have identified in Area 7, you don't have to spend it all. What we have done is set a limit. The fun part is, "How can we spend the least amount?"

At this point, list ALL of the possible expense, everything that might cost you money. What if the person you think can get you something for free or at a discount changes job, or simply just can't get it done for you right now? Don't let that be the end of a great idea! Plan for the expense now to see if you can manage without the help. Step by step, figure out what, and who, and how much. For our newspaper column, it will cost us $1,800 for the space in the paper. What other expenses are there? Will the rector write the column for free? Someone from the congregation? A freelance seminarian? How much might that cost? We could pay a seminarian $100 per column. That's $600, maximum. People in our congregation can review and edit. Any other expenses? Not that we can think of right now. Great, now we know that if we can get nothing to be discounted or for free, it will cost us $2,400, and that's below what we think we can raise. We are in good shape!

Area #9 Key metrics: Key metrics are the things we will look at and measure to figure out if our idea works. We generally overlook this because, in the church, we tend to focus on ASA (average Sunday attendance). However, when we dig a little deeper we can find metrics that really matter. It's worth taking some time to discuss what you are really trying to accomplish.

The Mission Canvas has already allowed us to consider a biweekly column rather than weekly. Our intended audience is recent retirees seeking meaning. How might we measure success? We could create a special section of the church website with the current and past columns. On that page, they can sign up for a newsletter that emails them the next column a day before publication. Some of the key metrics will be number of visits to the website and the number of people who subscribe to the newsletter. We could create a Facebook group where people can discuss the "Exploring Theology" columns. That becomes another metric: how many new people (not current members of the church) join the new group.

Something else happened. Our idea expanded from a column in the paper to a column that drives people to our website and to a new "Theology Explained" community. We hadn't thought about them before, but now they make perfect sense. The mission canvas has made our idea better!

Expanding the idea means that we need to consider possible costs associated with adding a new page to the website and maintaining our new Facebook group. Do we want to advertise our new group on Facebook to get other people from the area who are interested in the subject matter? How much will that cost?

You can do this

In early 2020, I had the opportunity to keynote and lead workshops about trying at the Winter Convocation for the Episcopal Diocese of Ohio. During one of my workshops, the youth who were present at the convocation came in to sit at the back of the room. They were killing time before the indoor waterpark opened. I knew that was their real goal.

As I talked through the steps of trying, I passed out copies of the Mission Canvas and walked the audience through all the steps. The youth were pretty well behaved, and I didn't think much about them until they left to the waterpark and we all waved goodbye.

A week or so after my visit, I got an email from the person who had invited me. The subject line read, "You will love this." This was the note:

> *This is the ministry plan a young man wrote in your morning workshop. Sorry it's a little hard to read. It's really wonderful. And I love the metric: "more babies crying."*

It turns out that a fourteen-year-old at one of the back tables was following along with my Mission Canvas conversation in the workshop, and he had an idea that he worked his way through. So, he filled it out. His idea? He wanted younger people to come to church, and he figured we'd know we have more younger people in church if we heard "more babies crying." If teenagers can do this work, then so can we, to build a better church for God.

Developing a Minimum Viable Prototype

An MVP helps determine the least thing that we can try to figure out if an idea has any merit. What's the smallest amount of money we can spend? How we can figure out if something is worth investing more time and money? The easiest way to do this is to focus on the key metrics from the Mission Canvas, because we have already indicated that these are the most important measures of success.

By calling them prototypes, we communicate that these ideas are not necessarily "forever," but something we're testing out. It changes the expectation of those who are involved in this process. For our purposes in the church and trying, there are two prototypes that will cover most of the ideas we'll develop. They are the low-fidelity prototype and the very limited run.

Low-fidelity prototype

A low-fidelity prototype is a very basic starting point to try out something. You were thinking of starting a social enterprise to earn revenue for the mission work of the church, and your idea is a cottage industry bakery. Most states have laws allowing cottage industries, meaning that you can use your own noncommercial kitchen to make baked goods as long as you follow some basic rules and have a cap on the allowed yearly revenue. A low-fidelity prototype would be to make a flyer ($20) that drove people to a website ($30) that said "Bakery coming soon!" and maybe gave people the opportunity to sign up for a newsletter. Then you spent $40 to run some Facebook ads targeted to the neighborhood of the church. For less than $100, you can gauge the interest in the social enterprise. If you get the word out and nobody comes to the website, it might mean there's not enough interest or too much competition already.

Very limited-run prototype

There are other times when you need to put something out there in its biggest form to see if it has legs. If your idea is more of an experience, you may want people to experience it to see if it works. So, if what you're considering is a contemporary worship service, then the way of testing it is to do it. Before you make a commitment to having a new contemporary service every week, why not try it for a time and see if it works? Advent and Lent are two very convenient short seasons right before Christmas and Easter. Those are perfect times with natural endings. If it works, then you can say popular demand made it a new regular thing. If it doesn't, then the ending was there from the get-go.

There are times when mixing the two will give you a prototype that fits your needs. You can do a low-fidelity version of something for a limited run. Maybe the cottage bakery will produce hot cross buns as a test. Conveniently, the buns are produced only around Lent and Easter. The bakery can be tested for a limited run with a special, and timely, product.

Instead of running our newspaper column weekly, we could do a limited run in the newspaper every other week. A low-fidelity version of the idea might be to publish them only on the website and run geographic ads targeting folks who are sixty-five plus on Facebook. In developing the prototype, and researching a bit more, and looking at costs and other factors, you might decide that the experiment would get more bang for the buck by being only on Facebook.

Don't be afraid to develop something that works for your idea. After all, that's what you are testing out. Stay focused on the key metrics and keep asking yourself, "What's the easiest, cheapest, fastest, way to get to these metrics and see if this idea is indeed a good one?"

In all of the decisions you are making, invite God to be with you and help you discern the best course of action. I have found that the

Holy Spirit is incredibly creative and wants to be part of this work. We invite the Holy Spirit and then listen to what the Spirit may be saying.

It's Time to Try!

You have the idea, you have the Mission Canvas, you know what you are looking for, and you have an MVP. It is now time to try your idea. So, try!

I have two pieces of advice: First, just keep moving forward. Ask yourself, "What's the very next step to take?" and keep moving forward. The list of next steps is actually your execution plan. Write many of the steps before you even start. You will find your rhythm. For the newspaper column idea, the very next step would be to see if we can work something out with the newspaper and ask the rector to write it. Once you have that, ask again, "What's the very next step to take?"

Second, remember that you will never get it perfect, so don't wait for that to happen. There are many times when we have to say, "That's good enough." Don't let perfection become a stumbling block. Get your idea out and make it better as you learn from the real world.

The Trying Cycle

The act of trying means you get out there and execute your idea. You do the thing you were planning to do. Well done! But there's actually a rhythm that most of us follows intuitively, the trying cycle.

First, you try your idea.

Second, you evaluate it. At some point data comes in that allows you to measure the idea against your key metrics, comparing reality with the expectation.

Third, based on the feedback you are getting, you refine the idea. This is called iteration. You make adjustments to get you closer to what you wanted to achieve.

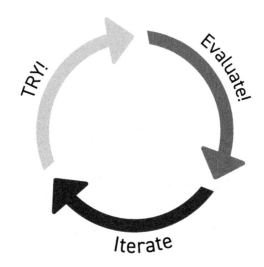

Fourth, you try again or end the trying. Based on the updates and iterations, you can either keep going with the newer version or you can decide to end the experiment.

How to evaluate

Evaluation is judging the reality of what happened with what you thought might happen. That's why the key metrics in the Mission Canvas are important. They give you something to measure against. Here are the key metrics for our newspaper column:

- 100 new unique visitors to our website
- 30 new email subscribers
- A 2 percent engagement rate on Facebook

All three of the metrics measure whether we are reaching new people. It is possible that even though we are targeting a particular age group, not all of the people we are reaching are newly retired, of course. But when you consider the columns are about the Good News of Jesus, does it really matter? The more, the merrier!

In evaluating, consider the resources it took to get these results. Is there something else that's effective and takes fewer resources? We might find that Facebook ads for columns on our website get the same results for less money than buying the space in the newspaper. (This is why the internet has challenged the business model for newspapers!)

Resources are more than money. Time and effort go into making sure this works. Is this something you can see your church doing for a while, or is it more trouble than it's worth? If it's not fun, try something else that your team will find enjoyable. Don't get stuck on one that makes you all miserable.

If you tried something and it did not work, that is not a big deal. There's a reason we went through the effort of creating the minimum viable prototype, so that you don't bet the house (or the church) on an idea. In fact, if you don't fail along the way, you may want to consider looking for ideas further outside the box.

To really get at these questions, the whole team participates in the evaluation. This is also a good opportunity to get others from the congregation who are not on the team to help out, which again creates more buy-in among the congregation. In doing this you may determine that while you may not have reached your key metrics, you nevertheless found something new that's very exciting.

A few years back before we started TryTank, I was working for the Episcopal Diocese of Los Angeles. As a relatively new priest, I wanted to reach my nieces and nephews. At the time, they were in their early twenties. Then I had an idea. I would create some short videos (under three minutes) that would be mini-sermons on the Sunday gospel. But rather than just me speaking, we'd edit in some quick, funny videos from YouTube that could help make my point. So, if I talked about Jesus on a boat, we'd cut away to a video of a boat. When I talked about the Good Shepherd, we'd cut away to video of sheep "ba-aaa-ing" all over the place. Thanks to Chris Tumilty, my partner in crime who edited the videos, they came out great!

The key metric of the experiment was pretty simple: Did my nieces and nephews watch the videos, and did they like them? I wasn't trying to get them to come to church on Sunday or to have a life-altering transformation. I just wanted them to watch the videos.

They did not work as intended. Of the 20,000 + views that added up to more than 60,000 minutes of the gospel being seen on Facebook, none were my nieces and nephews. So ended the season of videos.

But then something interesting happened. Several of the folks who reached out to me on Facebook to find out why the videos had stopped being produced were communion ministers who visited the sick at home. They found the videos to be an incredible resource! They could read the day's gospel, show the mini-sermon, talk about it, and then give communion. It felt like a liturgy to them. Obviously, that was not one of our key metrics since we had no idea that the need existed. We only discovered it when the experiment failed. TryTank is now formally trying "Home Sermons" as an experiment to see if indeed there are enough people who would use them.

When I was in seminary in New York City, I had the privilege of seeing a friend ordained at the Church of St. Mary the Virgin. The preacher was an older priest with an awesome British accent. At one point in his sermon, he turned to my friend and said: "Always work and push . . . remember that you cannot destroy the church of God . . . people much more powerful than us have tried and failed. So, us trying to do good will never destroy the church." I give you those words as a reminder. We won't break the church trying something that may seem a bit "out there."

So, try. And do it with abandon.

You only need five

What if I told you that when you are trying something you only need five users to see if it will work? It's true! This is another concept from the business world that is incredibly useful in our work.

It turns out that some people[2] way smarter than I am created a formula to prove this point: N (1-(1-L) n). Some of you right now are saying, "Okay, I'm out . . . he never mentioned algebra was needed." Stay with me. I can't read that either, but I can explain what it means.

Let's say you have a new gadget—a new pen. When you share that pen with someone and ask for feedback, they will give you about 33 percent of anything you could learn about your new pen. When you share it with a second someone, they will tell you all the things the first someone shared and a few new insights. At this point, you have gained about 50 percent of what you can learn from the users. By the third someone, you are at about 66 percent of what you can learn. By the time you get to the fifth someone, you will have learned about 85 percent of what you can expect to learn. From here on out, every new someone you show it to will only give you information you already know and once in a while, a small little something you hadn't yet heard. With 85 percent of the possible feedback you have enough information to make decisions about what is next for the experiment.

This is what that looks like:

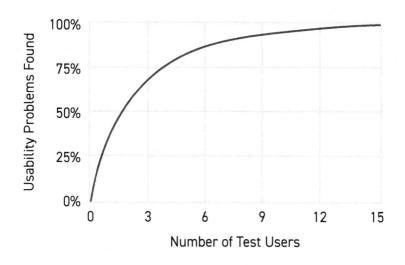

2. You can check out Jakob Nielsen's fascinating short article on this here: https://www.nngroup.com/articles/why-you-only-need-to-test-with-5-users/

The same is true of our ongoing experiment. You could take one of the "Exploring Theology" columns and share it with some people to get their feedback, particularly about how it gives a sense of meaning. By the time you hear back from five readers, you will know pretty well if the article is doing what you want, and how to adjust appropriately.

Sunk cost fallacy

In behavioral economics, there is a theory called the "sunk cost fallacy." Briefly stated, "Individuals commit the sunk cost fallacy when they continue a behavior or endeavor as a result of previously invested resources (time, money or effort)."[3] Don't feel bad if you have ever done this, we all fall into this way of thinking. We're wired to believe that the time or money we already have invested into something should be factored into our current decision making. This logic is flawed.

The sunk cost fallacy is one of my main takeaways from business school. It seems that every class we took covered the concept and put it deep into our brains. There is a time when you simply have to ask, "Are we going to keep investing in something even though we know the outcome will not be what we want simply because we already have put money into it?" You may know it by its less academic term, "throwing good money after bad."

The concept of sunk cost is not just for business. I have seen it violated in the arts, the nonprofit sector, and in the church. In the church, we really value tradition, and tradition is one of the easiest ways to stop looking at whether something works/is worth doing/we even like doing it. We do it because—say it with me—"we've always done it." When experimenting, it is especially important to know when to pull the plug on something.

---

3. "Sunk Cost Fallacy," Behavioral Economics, https://www.behavioraleconomics.com/resources/mini-encyclopedia-of-be/sunk-cost-fallacy/.

There is one TryTank experiment in particular that illustrates this point. We announced an experiment called "Drunk Bible" based on the hit Comedy Central show *Drunk History*. The concept is fairly simple; you get someone drunk and get them to tell a story from history. Since the story will, um, take a few detours as the person gets more drunk, it becomes pretty funny. You then get actors to reenact the story as told by the drunk person. It really is funny, and I thought it might be a good way to reach younger people who might otherwise not be at all interested in the Bible. One of my nephews (yes, from the "didn't watch my videos on YouTube" nephews) even said he'd pay to see this.

After we announced the experiment, we heard back from many followers of our work who were hurt by us having to resort to alcohol to bring young people to the Bible. They were right, not just in that truth, but that some people would be disappointed and hurt that the church did it this way. We decided that this was not something we wanted to do. (We also adopted a "first, do no harm" philosophy for our experiments.)

Instead, we pivoted, and we created "Street Bible." In this new iteration of the idea, we'd get the funny versions of Bible stories from random people by doing "person-on-the-street" interviews. However, along the way, we lost sight of who we wanted as our audience and the end product showed that. It simply wasn't good.

In evaluating, we considered trying to market the videos via Facebook ads and see if would catch on with any group. We showed the videos around to a few as a way of early testing. It clearly showed that there was really no "there" there. And so, we got to the question: Do we keep investing in this because we've already invested time and money into it, or do we call it a day?

For us, we concluded that if we thought getting this right it would move the needle and more people would find their way to God and life as a follower of Christ, then maybe it'd be worthwhile, but we have other, more focused experiments that have a greater chance of being successful. So ended another experiment. That's why we call it experimenting.

—— FIELD NOTES ——

Here are some of the experiments that are in development as of this writing:

Facebook "Opens"

Design question: How might we reach people who are open to the Christian message but currently have no church relationship?

The idea: Research shows that there are many people who are open to the Christian message but are not part of a church. They are not against church for some philosophical, moral, or theological reason. As a matter of fact, they like the Christian message. It is just that attending church is not necessarily important to them. They are living out their faith in everyday life. They are younger (around thirty) and maybe are just starting a family. We decided that rather than calling them "unchurched," which sounds as if they are missing something, we would call them "Opens."

In our research, we also discovered that Facebook has a tool to create lookalike audiences. As long as you have a page with a hundred or more "likes," Facebook is able to find other people who are like them. They do this by looking at all the data points that they have on those people who "liked" a page and then looking for statistical anomalies. In other words, if you took a random sample of a hundred people, how many of them are likely to share a data point of liking the color "green"? Let's say it's 0.05 percent. If your group happens to have 5 percent who like the color green, then this is a statistical anomaly and a unique trait of people who happen to like your page. If you do this with several of those data points, what you end up with is a kind of unique DNA of the group.

What if we created a Facebook page that puts out content aimed at this group of people who are open but not in a church and got many of them to like our new page? The research also shows that many of these people are very interested in social justice issues. Which makes sense if you look at the people who turned out for something like the economic justice–focused Bernie Sanders presidential campaign, rallies about climate change, or demonstrations for Black Lives Matter. These younger people are living their faith by seeking justice. They are like the prophets of old and don't even know it!

In another experiment, we tried Facebook lookalike audiences for the first time. When the organization put up a normal post, they had a 3 percent engagement rate. Keep in mind that a regular post on Facebook will have less than 1 percent engagement. So, not bad, right? When the same post was in the form of a video (which was what we were testing), the engagement rate shot up to 10 percent. That is simply amazing! We had three times the engagement by having a video. Nice! Then we asked Facebook to find lookalikes to the page we were using. That page had more than four thousand "likes" so there was a lot of data for Facebook to mine. We set a specific geographic area and shared the video post. We had a 48 percent engagement! For these people who hadn't heard of the organization but shared the same interests and values, this was awesome new content. It was then that we realized the power of lookalikes.

Next, we hired a PR firm to create content for a new page on Facebook called "Justice IS Faith." We hope the Opens will identify with the content. And we will promote the very shareable posts mostly to women who are in their early thirties and who also like social justice organizations and do not "like" a church page.

This experiment has tremendous potential. Imagine if we are able to get the DNA for people who are open to the Christian message but not affiliated with a congregation? With that DNA we could ask Facebook to find people who are just like them but in a very specific geographic area—like the neighborhood around your church. We could share with them information about the congregation and its values related to social justice. The end result is not that they will all show up to your church this Sunday. Following the basics of marketing, which are "know, like, and trust" (where a person needs to know your church before they can like it and eventually trust it, then move toward calling a church home), this is the first step.

I feel this experiment really has a chance to help us reach new people.

Planting by Radio

Design question: How might we reach Spanish-speaking members of a neighborhood to form community as a precursor to planting a new congregation?

The idea: One of the most often used methods for planting a new church is to put a missioner in a geographic area and have them build relationships, one at a time. After a while a small community will form, and they will eventually be ready to become a worshipping community. This tried method takes time and resources. Is there another way of building community that takes fewer resources?

Hispanics are still very much listeners of local radio. According to the Nielsen folks, radio is the source of news Hispanics trust the most and radio is part of their daily lives. What if we bought a half hour of radio time on a local Spanish-speaking radio station to run a weekly show on Sunday mornings? Could we form a community this way that over time would come together for worship?

A half hour on radio costs a few hundred dollars a week. For our purposes, we don't need to have thousands of people listening, we just need a few hundred. Personally (and I don't yet have any research to prove this, just anecdotal stories), I believe that the theology of the Episcopal Church is very much in line with the theology of most Hispanics in this country. Like most of us, they tend to stick with the faith tradition they grew up with rather than seek out something new. But what if the something new came to them via a format they really enjoy?

In conceiving the show, we feel it should be a call-in style show that is entertaining but serious about theology. The hosts should be funny yet empathetic and compassionate. Remember *Car Talk* on NPR? While it was about cars, it was also very fun to listen to each week. This is what we are looking to create—a show about God and deep theological issues in an open, "we don't have all the answers" kind of way. Again, we are following the basics of marketing (know, like, and trust). We'll be measuring how many people trust us enough over time to give us their cell phone number to get a weekly prayer by text.

As of right now, we are looking at trying this in three states to get a true sense of whether this is something that could work. If it does, it certainly also has the potential to offer a new way of planting a Spanish-speaking congregation.

Prayer Puppets

Design question: How might we offer Christian formation to young kids who are not attending church on a regular basis?

The idea: The new norm in our world is that when a new family starts to attend a church, they are likely to show up once every four to six weeks. With so many other things going on in their lives, they try to spread themselves around. It's just the new reality. In their minds, they basically don't want a month to go by without going to church. If they have young kids who they send to Sunday school when they are in church, it means that the kids are getting a lesson every few weeks. And if those lessons build on each other, they are getting episode one and then episode five. In the end, they're not getting all they can.

What if we created a streamed show that kids could watch? What would it look and feel like? We actually began by asking, if Mr. Rogers were around today and his show was about Christian formation, what would it look like? We eventually got rid of the live person, but the idea kept much of the feel of Mr. Rogers. We went with puppets. Imagine a Christian *Sesame Street*.

We are aiming to make the show about 5–6 minutes and hope that, if it works, it could be a weekly show. Each episode covers a theme. The first three are faith, hope, and love (Saint Paul would be proud!). Each theme has its own original song. The colorful puppets look great! The puppeteers are experts and we have signed on with a production company to make sure that it has a professional look.

This ministry is aimed at kids two to five years old, and in the style of children's TV, it will use repetition to teach. While the themes will change each week, the show aims to teach three things: (1) there is a God, (2) you are beloved by God, and (3) you can pray to God.

Following the example of Mr. Rogers, it is meant to be a gentle show. It will live within its own app so that parents don't have to worry about them wandering far from the show into other content. The songs will also be able to be played by themselves. If people like and subscribe to the show, it can find its way to be a new ministry. With a small subscription price of, say, $4 a month for four new episodes, the show could go into production as a self-sustaining entity.

Since the population of the United States is 70 percent Christian, that means that there are about 230 million Christians here. How many of those are grandparents who'd like to see their grandkids have access to the Prayer Puppets? We're eager to see how this turns out.

Remember that these are in development during the writing of this book. By the time you read this, we will know more. Be sure to check out the TryTank website (www.TryTank.org).

6↻→

WARNING:
It Will Seem Long, and You Will Fail—and That's Awesome!

Congratulations! At this point, you have gained insights, come up with ideas, and actually executed one of those ideas. Along the way, you have gotten buy-in from the congregation and have evaluated how things are going. It's working beautifully, right? Then it's time we had The Talk.

The In-Between Time

Have you ever gone on a great road trip? Imagine one with me now. You are in a convertible (Hey, why not? We are imagining here!) and you are going to travel from Miami to Atlanta. When you first start on I-95 in Miami, everything is awesome. You have the special playlist you created for just this trip. It's got all of your favorite fast-moving songs. There's no traffic. The wind of the passing miles is hitting your hair. It's an amazing feeling.

Two hours later, when you are stuck in traffic around Palm Beach, you are still in a decent mood. The music is keeping you going (or is it the coffee?). It's just a little slower now.

Two hours after that, you've slowed down again due to an accident, and you decide to put the top on the convertible because it looks like the afternoon rain showers Florida is known for are coming soon. Your mood isn't great.

An hour later you're near Orlando in standstill traffic. The rain is worse than you imagined, and you have turned off the music to concentrate on the road. It's super humid and you are thinking to yourself that this is not the road trip you envisioned. Worst of all, you are only about halfway there. Sigh . . . you are now in the in-between time.

Some ten hours later you make it to Atlanta. You are beat. You wonder why you did this in the first place, but now you are there and the next day your energy is back because you reached your destination. And it all seems worth it, because you made it!

Friends, not everything will go according to plan. It will take longer than you think and sometimes you'll feel like you're doing all the work. The good news is that you know this going in!

You will probably not have the same excitement you felt when you first got the idea and got others to share in your enthusiasm and join in. When you are planning something to try, it's like the start of the road trip, with the wind in your hair and the music blasting. But it takes longer, and a person who said they'd do something flakes out, and it seems like it's never going to work no matter what. And then, the energy you had for the idea is all gone. Somehow, if you stick with it you eventually will get there. And it will all have been worth the effort.

Here's how you can prepare for this in-between time:

1. *Be aware:* Just knowing that it's very likely that this in-between time will happen is a huge boost to your energy reserves when it does happen. This in-between time is when most projects are abandoned and fail. Be aware and prepare yourself mentally for this.

2. *Make it spiritual:* Remember that we are doing this for the greater glory of God. So, when it starts to get long and hard and it seems like it'll never happen, pray! When you get to problems that you don't know how to handle, give them over to God. When it gets extra-long, just step aside and ask God to take over for a bit. Pope Saint John XXIII was sometimes really worried about the church and all the problems it faced. But right before bed, he'd say "It's your Church, God. I'm going to bed!"[1] If a saint can do it, so can we!

3. *Team works!* I am a firm believer that the reason Jesus sent out his disciples two by two is because he knew about the in-between time. Jesus knew that we'd have "those" days, and to handle them, it's easier with a buddy. When we work as a team we can hold each other up when things are not going well and when the in-between is longer than we want, thought, or can bear alone.

A Word on Failure

It would be odd to write a whole book about trying new things if I didn't take a moment to talk about those times when you will fail. Note I didn't say "might" but "will." Let's be super clear about this right now. Even if you follow all the steps and do everything correctly, there will be times when a new thing just doesn't work out. That's just life.

Unfortunately, because we are doing this work for the church (and God), I think that we put too much pressure on it being perfect, and that if it doesn't work, we have somehow let God down. It's quite the opposite! I believe that when we are trying for God and we fail, that's a holy failure and a good part of our spiritual practice.

1. Philip Kosloski, "When Falling Asleep, Pray This Prayer to Rest in Peace," Aleteia (blog), March 31, 2019, https://aleteia.org/2019/03/31/when-falling -asleep-pray-this-prayer-to-rest-in-peace/.

We can also be embarrassed by failing. That's normal and something we just have to accept. But when we own our good faith effort, even when it fails, we actually take away some of the embarrassment from it. I love telling the story about Spin Church exactly because it's a failure. We hope that TryTank can model for the church that failure is a normal part of trying.

The history of the church is filled with people trying for God and failing. Most of them are saints now. Sure, some of those saints are also martyrs, but I don't think any of our ideas here will cause any of us to become martyrs! In fact, what this process does for the new idea is two important things.

First, in following this process, you are less likely to fail due to something you could or should have seen coming. Getting the insights and doing the research and input from the group lead to ideas that are stronger and built on a solid foundation. That's great!

Second, having spent time getting buy-in and sharing the process along the way means that even if one idea fails, people will already be on board and less likely to say, "I told you so!" When we ended the Spin Church experiment and called it one that did not work, it took only fifty-seven minutes (less than an hour!) from the announcement before I got an email saying, "I knew that would never work." Most people, however, will recognize that there was a process and that the idea seemed worth trying and that it just didn't work. More likely than not, you will hear people encourage you on to the next time.

From a pastoral perspective, let me just add that God does not, never has, and never will demand perfection or success. Our souls are not on the line here. God only asks that we be faithful in the work we do and that we do it in a loving, moral, and ethical way. That's it.

Failing is part of the work and we can learn from those times as well. Even if the learning is "Well, we won't do that again," the next time you try something, that new idea will be informed by the one that didn't work. In all of this, trust that God is indeed very much present.

Sidebar: Unlock Your Creativity

Often when I am teaching this framework for trying in the church people will comment that I am super creative but that they, poor souls, are *not* creative. This got me wondering if indeed this was true. Was this work of trying relegated to the few who were creative?

When I was going through the ordination process, I had to take a lot of psychological tests: a really long multiple-choice test of around six hundred questions, some of those "What does this ink blot look like to you?" and lots of talking with a psychologist. In the end, I passed (showing the flaws in the system, right?) but I also discovered that I'm a divergent thinker. The psychologist said it meant that "If we're on a sinking boat, I am not letting you out of my sight." It turns out that most people, once they make a decision, start to block other possibilities and focus on just the one. People like me, with divergent thinking, will continue to see possibilities until the very last moment. I will grant you that I have a unique approach to this work.

However, I looked into whether this way of thinking affected my creativity, and for the record, just because I see more options does not mean that they're all good. Most are not. The research leads to the same conclusion: anyone can be creative.[2]

I started to do some regular exercises to become more creative. These exercises are just the tip of the iceberg. You can Google "how to be more creative" and you will find 3.180 billion (that's right, with a "B") results. Go ahead, indulge!

---

2. Ben Plomion, "Creativity Is for Everyone," *Forbes* (blog), June 22, 2018, https://www.forbes.com/sites/forbescommunicationscouncil/2018/06/22/creativity-is-for-everyone/#2ae22f7853f8.

Flash Fiction

Write a short story in just a hundred words. You don't need to be Hemingway to do this. If you don't share the stories with anyone, you won't be constrained by thinking that you have to write something good. Go ahead, write something bad! This is a great exercise since it forces your brain to go through a story arc in 100 words. It can be lots of fun.

Thirty Circles

On a while sheet of paper, start anywhere you want and draw a circle. Maybe about an inch in diameter (t it does not have to be perfect). Now turn that circle into an object. Maybe a face or a baseball or a pizza. Keep going until you have thirty circles on the sheet. It'll get tougher, but it's always interesting to see what you come up with, since toward the end you'll need to get really creative.

Go for a Walk

If you are sitting with a question and want more creative answers to it, take a break and go for a nice stroll. A leisurely walk will get your blood moving and that allows you to think of new creative solutions. I don't know how, but this seems to always work for me. There are times when I don't even realize that I am thinking through a question and then I'll go for my daily exercise and out of the blue come new solutions. Those are always surprising!

Sleep on It

If you want to use your sleep time to think more about possible solutions, make sure that the last thing you do before closing your eyes at night is to think through the question. Neurologists tell us that our brains will then keep working on the question while we sleep. It won't affect your dreams; it's just your subconscious mind working while you're sleeping. Since you are not interrupted and it can focus, you will get some good answers. I also use this as an opportunity to ask God to be present. Make sure that you have a small notebook near your bed so that you can write down what you were thinking about immediately after you wake up.

Keep an Idea Book / Sketchbook

I encourage you to keep an idea notebook. It's basically a place where you can jot down some quick thoughts or where you can write your flash fiction. It might even be where you sketch! Trust me, I "sketch" about as well as I speak French: you might be able to tell what it is, but more likely it's just sitting out there, unidentified. The sketches are for me.

Set Aside Time

This last one is not so much an exercise as it is something you should strive to do when you are trying to be creative. Find a place where you can be without disruptions and without anything to take your mind off the task. If you're on your computer, turn off other programs that have pop-up notifications (like Outlook). Put your phone away. The biggest killer of creativity is interruptions, so try to minimize those.

7

Using This Book
as a Leadership Team

Design thinking is a powerful framework to use for a church leadership or vestry[1] retreat. If you are going outside the box to become the congregation God is calling you to be in the world today, this is a great way to do it.

The Episcopal Church Foundation has many great resources available for free on their website to help you run a top-notch retreat.[2] This section will cover how to incorporate this framework into the retreat. The one assumption this makes is that the whole vestry is acting as a team. It is especially important that the facilitator makes sure that everyone is heard, and that one or two people are not pushing through their ideas.

While many resources suggest having an outside facilitator, since this book provides a framework for the retreat, that's not necessary. The facilitator will be the one who makes sure the meetings happen as

---

1. In the Episcopal Church, the vestry is the governing board of a congregation. Consider this to mean a leadership team for your church.
2. You can find many here: https://www.ecfvp.org/blogs/3548/5-vestry-retreat-resources.

efficiently as possible. They will also be the point person for information coming in and out from the group.

To maximize use of this framework in a retreat, I suggest breaking it down into phases, much like our steps for trying:

Phase One: Generating Insights (and design question)
Phase Two: Developing Ideas (the overnight)
Phase Three: Trying

Phase One: Insights (and Design Question)

I recommend that the retreat actually begin two months (or eight weeks) out from the overnight event. Make sure that everyone has a copy of this book so that they understand the framework and how it works.

Get together for two or three hours on a Saturday to discern your design question and then begin the insight work by dividing up the research that you'd like to do. Take time with this conversation.

In preparation for the meeting, ask all members to spend some time at home doing a SWOT analysis (Strengths, Weaknesses, Opportunities, and Threats)[3] of the congregation. There are many resources online about how to do this, but it's not rocket science, just sit and think through each of the four sections.

When you gather, begin the day with prayer. Then spend the first thirty minutes with everyone sharing their SWOT analysis of the congregation. On four sheets of paper on the wall, one for each category, record the answers given. Everyone should be ready to discuss their assessment.

For the next hour or so, concentrate on the opportunities section of the analysis. The strengths, weaknesses, and threats are left up because they inform our opportunities. This part works best as a conversation, the less formal, the more laughter, the better. Be open.

---

3. You can get a good overview of the process at https://en.wikipedia.org/wiki/SWOT_analysis.

Toward the end of the hour, start to zero in on which opportunities the group feels most called to explore. Eventually, settle on one to turn into your design question. The question is still "What if?" and not yet "How might we . . . ?"

Remember that just because you don't pursue an idea now does not mean that you never will. It just means that one is taking priority. You can always come back. While it is possible to explore two different opportunities and then decide, I don't recommend it. Choose one at a time so that you can really give your all to the project.

When each member leaves at the end of this meeting, they should be clear on what the design question is, and what portion of the insight phase will be their responsibility. Will they be looking at secondary research? Will they be having conversations with people? Will they be observing? Whatever it is, they should be very clear about their task. Set up a Dropbox (or similar) to collect the data so that everyone has access to it. As soon as you set it up, add the design question, tasks, and deadlines.

Four weeks after the first meeting (which is also four weeks before the overnight retreat), have a check-in meeting to see what you are learning and what needs more investigation.

Phase Two: Ideas (the Overnight)

When you first gather, after your prayer period, begin with thirty minutes of playing some game (maybe one of the creativity exercises from the previous chapter). This will help establish the playful mindset that is so important for the ideas phase.

With the design question front and center (maybe on a flip chart), begin to share all of the insights you have gathered from each team member. Take notes of the insights and themes. You'll want to do this before and after dinner. Just share the stories.

Before everyone goes to bed, invite the Holy Spirit in prayer to inspire your minds and hearts in the work you are doing together.

Encourage everyone to go to sleep thinking on the design question and the insights. I know this may sound odd, but I have found that creativity really flourishes if we invite the Holy Spirit to illumine our minds overnight. Trust me!

When you reconvene after breakfast, run through several of the ideation exercises in this book, especially the brainstorm. If your group is more than seven people, split up into two smaller groups. Brainstorming really benefits from a smaller size. When you regather into the larger group you can merge ideas and see themes to discover commonalities.

Before you break for lunch, decide which one or two ideas you want to move forward. These are the ideas from which you will decide what to try first. I recommend only doing this if your group is large enough to break into two managing groups that can run the idea as their own experiment.

After lunch, work on a Mission Canvas for each of the ideas. Make sure you go through each area. Finally, you will want to decide which idea you will try and begin to develop an execution plan. Remember to keep asking: "What's the very next step?" since that will be your plan. Make sure that part of your plan is to share back to the congregation so that you are always working to get their buy-in of the process and the ideas.

Phase Three: Trying

After the retreat and with your plan in hand, start taking those very next steps to trying. Set up regular check-in points so that you can evaluate based on the metrics you articulated in the Mission Canvas. Then make your decisions accordingly.

A great benefit of doing this as a vestry is that, in theory, the whole leadership team is in on the process and have bought in to the work. Make sure to keep and have accessible the initial SWOT analysis, all of the research that generated insights, to the many ideas, to the Mission

Canvas that you used. All of these documents will allow you to go back and see what led to the choices that were made and to share it with anyone who has questions.

One final thought: since we are always looking for ways of inviting God into this work, try to come up with a few meaningful prayer breaks during the retreat. Consider having a candle lit during the work to represent the presence of God.

FINAL THOUGHTS: CELEBRATING EXPERIMENTATION

I'd like to retell you a story. In the fall of 2018, I was officially offered the job to become director of TryTank, the brand new experimental lab for church growth and innovation. As I looked over the offer letter, I was incredibly excited by this prospect of doing this new thing in the church, but I had one reservation that I needed to clear up.

I asked each of the deans of Virginia Theological Seminary and General Theological Seminary the same question: "When we look back in three or five years, how will we know that we have succeeded?" I was actually afraid that they would say something like "Well, we will have found the silver bullet" or "Because we will have saved the church." If something even remotely close to that was the answer, I was out. There's just no way I was capable of taking on anything like that.

Kurt Dunkle, the dean and president at General, simply said, "Because we will have failed more often that we have succeeded."

Ian Markham, the dean and president at Virginia, said, "Because we'll have hundreds of experiments that we will have tried." I immediately signed my letter and took the job.

There is a reason why we use the term "experiment" for each of the ideas that we try. Much like a scientific laboratory, we want to make it clear that nothing we are trying is a sure thing. Rather, all of them are experiments and while we want them to work, the possibility of failing is just as likely.

Friends, we need to celebrate experimentation in the church. Not just because in doing so we will find new ways of being the church the world needs today. We need to experiment so that we can keep looking for God's revelation in the world. As comedian Gracie Allen said, "Never place a period where God has placed a comma." If we believe that our God is still active in the world today, then that same God is still revealing Godself to us, but it is up to us to keep looking.

Experimenting allows us to find new ministries that enable us to do our work better. The lost sheep sought by the Good Shepherd are still out there and we need to keep reaching out in new ways to find them.

This is why prayer is such an important part of this work. I encourage you to celebrate your experiments by incorporating them into some of your Sunday worshipping celebrations. As the work begins, commission the team members in church. Begin team meetings with prayer each time. As updates become available, announce them from the pulpit. When an idea has been selected, share the good news and what that will look like as part of a service. When you are actually trying the idea, make sure that it incorporates prayer. And when something doesn't work, make sure you honor the work and effort that went into it with some prayers as well.

May God bless you in this holy work. Now, go try!

A Short Commissioning

Presider	There is one Body and one Spirit;
People	There is one hope in God's call to us;
Presider	One Lord, one Faith, one Baptism;
People	One God and Father of all.
Presider	The Lord be with you.
People	And also with you.
Presider	Let us pray.

Gracious God, you sent your Son Jesus to proclaim to all the Good News of your Kingdom, and through him inspired individuals to sow the seeds of your Church: Help us as we continue this work. Empower N., your servants, and all who support them, and give them the gifts to accomplish your will; all of which we ask through Jesus our Savior. Amen.

Read: Luke 10:1–9 (Pray the Lord of the harvest to send laborers)

O God, we praise you for the redemption of the world through the death and resurrection of Jesus the Christ. We thank you for pouring out your Spirit upon us, making some apostles, some prophets, some evangelists, some pastors and teachers to equip your people for the building up of the Body of Christ. Bless this new work that we undertake, that your Name may be glorified, now and for ever. Amen.